Paris

ON AIR
A MEMOIR

OLIVER GEE
HOST OF THE AWARD-WINNING PODCAST THE EARFUL TOWER

PRAISE FOR OLIVER GEE

"Oliver Gee has the talent of finding love and humour in Paris's smallest details. He definitely is one of our greatest Parisian voices." - **CAROLINE DE MAIGRET**, model and author of How to Be Parisian Wherever You Are.

"The Earful Tower is one of the few Paris podcasts I always listen to. Oliver Gee is very engaging, and presents a different side of Paris, from his personal perspective, with panache, and wit." - **DAVID LEBOVITZ**, author of My Paris Kitchen and Drinking French.

"He's the Crocodile Dundee of Paris." - **JOHN BAXTER**, author of The Most Beautiful Walk in The World and A Year in Paris.

"What I value about Oliver and his Earful Tower is his openness to all things Parisian - from the historically obscure to the au courant cafés - and the curiosity that drives him to find fascinating Parisian details. A fresh, entertaining voice and the best on the Paris scene." - **CARA BLACK**, author of the Aimée Leduc mystery novels.

"Oliver's enthusiasm is contagious, his energy apparently inexhaustible. He even has a wonderful sense of humor. I will flatter myself here by wondering why Oliver Gee and his love of Paris remind me of myself and my own passion those many years ago, when I arrived as a young man in The City of Light. Vive la République, vive l'amour!" - **DAVID DOWNIE**, author of Paris, Paris: Journey into the City of Light and Paris to the Pyrenees.

Earful Tower Publishing

ISBN: 978-1-09830-199-6 (Paperback)
ISBN: 978-1-09830-200-9 (eBook)

Library of Congress Control Number: 00000000000

Front cover image by Lina Nordin Gee.

First printing edition 2020.

Get in touch with the author: contact@theearfultower.com
www.theearfultower.com

CONTENTS

INTRODUCTION

The ring weighed heavy in my pocket as we stepped into the cold Paris night. And it wasn't heavy because it was big - it definitely wasn't big. It was more heavy in the sense that I felt a crushing pressure from my imminent proposal.

We were leaving a Left Bank party and were set to walk to Hemingway's bar in the Ritz. My plan was to stop on a bridge somewhere along the Seine River, to ask her to marry me, then to continue to the hotel bar. I double checked the directions discreetly. A twenty-minute walk, fairly straightforward; but as we stepped out into the crisp evening air on rue de l'Odeon, a light rain began to fall.

"Let's grab a cab," she said.

A cab? No, we have to walk, I thought. *I can't propose to her in a taxi. Can I?*

"Ah, we don't need a taxi, Paris is beautiful when it rains," I responded.

"I can't even walk, my shoes are too small," she pleaded. "Can't we get a cab?"

Should I throw it all in? Postpone the proposal? No. The timing is perfect.

"Don't be silly, we'll never find a cab," I lied. "And the Ritz is just a short walk anyway," I lied again.

We set off in the rain, or I suppose you could call it a light drizzle. Almost a mist, really. And we made it down through the Christmas lights on the Left Bank to the Seine. But I could hardly breathe. The One Ring was weighing me down.

Where's the Pont Neuf bridge? That's a romantic one, I thought.

"The Pont Neuf? That's way behind us, it's the wrong way," she answered.

Oh God, I'm thinking out loud. The ring is controlling me. I need to regain control. Find a bridge. Get to the middle. Ask her to marry me.

The nearest bridge was the famed Pont des Arts, but even late on a Sunday night, there were still pedestrians crossing it. Through the drizzle I swear I could see a man down on one knee. No good! Too much of a cliché.

What's that next one up the road? It looks nice. It looks old. It looks romantic. Must get to bridge. Must destroy the ring…

We got to the old stone crossing, the Pont du Carrousel, which led to the Louvre museum on the Right Bank. The bridge was empty, not a person or a car in sight. It was perfect.

I had to ask her right then. That, or I had to cast the ring into the Seine and be rid of it forever. I turned and looked at her. Hair wet from the drizzling rain. Eyes glowing golden from the reflected light of the Paris lampposts. Feet swollen from the undersized shoes. Yes, the moment was right.

"My precious," I began. *Weird, I'd never called her that before.* "We've been in Paris for three years now, but it still feels like those first nights: clueless, hopeless, and penniless. Those were the best nights of my life. And I want to spend the rest of my nights - and the rest of my days - with you. Will you marry me?"

I'd stopped breathing about two minutes earlier. I swayed. Time stopped. Then I heard her say yes, four times to be sure, and I breathed again. I slipped the ring on her finger: the weight was lifted and she kissed me in the Paris rain. We moved on towards the Ritz Hotel, with the lights of Place Vendôme leading the way. This promised to be the start of something beautiful.

Now, if I'd have known that on our honeymoon six months later I'd be lying by the road in the French countryside, in agony from a mysterious disease, I'd have thrown the damned ring in the river and jumped in after it.

But I'm getting ahead of myself…

CHAPTER ONE

———

A dream apartment in Paris,
a new life as a journalist,
and a Swedish woman.

1.1 The arrival

Now that you know how the story ends, it's only fair that you know how it begins. And it's a lot less romantic, I can tell you. In fact, if you're only here for the happy stories, you should skip this section. You should also skip chapter 1.5, 2.7, and maybe even 8.2 if you don't like the sound of Lyme Disease.

Anyway, it wasn't love that brought me to Paris, it was hate. Evil, even. It was the terrorist attack on the Charlie Hebdo newspaper in January 2015. On the day of the attack, I was winding up my time as a journalist in Sweden, writing a fluff piece about a viral cartoon. I was putting the finishing touches on the story when one of the senior editors announced that Charlie Hebdo had been attacked, apparently by terrorists.

I heard him say it from the other side of the room and I wondered what a Charlie Hebdo was. I searched online for "Charlie Ebdo" - without the H, based on his pronunciation - and found it was France's main satirical magazine. Its unrelenting shots at religion had left it with enemies abroad. The editor came over to my desk and asked how soon I could be ready to go to Paris.

"For Charlie Hebdo?" I asked, feigning that I was already on top of the story. "I can go right away."

"Take the next plane," he responded. "You can come back for your luggage later."

It wasn't meant to happen like that, but that's the nature of the news. You can't plan around it, and I'd soon learn this was especially true in France. The way it was meant to happen was that I'd head to Paris on a one-way ticket a month or so later. During this final month in Sweden I had planned to cram the entirety of France, its news, and its language into my head so I'd arrive ready to tackle the country as a reporter. After all, like I said in my job interview, I was certain my university-level French would come back like lightning. And how hard could it be to get up to speed with French news?

As it turned out, it took far longer than a month or two to understand the French, their language, and their culture. And I had no time for it anyway. France, and especially Paris, was getting its first taste of a series of horrific attacks, and the world wanted to know what was happening. I rammed some clothes into a suitcase and took the next flight out of Stockholm.

Even though what followed was technically my arrival in Paris, it never felt like it. I had my head buried in the news and didn't stop to smell the pastry. And it was made worse by the fact that I was desperately unprepared to cover the Charlie Hebdo attack as a journalist. I had zero context about how it would affect life for Parisians because I wasn't a Parisian. I was no different from the hundreds of other foreign correspondents sent to cover the story. People call it parachute journalism, where reporters are dropped into a location then pulled out again before anyone knows what has truly happened. I felt like I was a parachute journalist too, even though I was set to stay in Paris long after the parachute was packed away.

The attack had taken place at the Charlie Hebdo offices in the 11th arrondissement, a trendy part of the city that I'd never heard of before. I'd never read a Charlie Hebdo newspaper and at the time I wouldn't have understood it if I had tried. But I was there, talking to people on the street and getting their reactions to the attacks, which had left 17 people dead - mostly at the Charlie Hebdo office. But while I lacked the context, the truth is that journalists don't need to be experts on a topic to write about it. Anyone can ask what happened and record a reaction. And you can always fill in the context with a bit of extra time or a few phone calls. That's how all the foreign correspondents were doing it. But for me, in those first days after the attack, I was realizing just how unprepared I was for a new life as a reporter in Paris.

That weekend I joined in with the masses of Parisians who marched in solidarity over the attacks. They were putting on a defiant face against evil and it was spectacular to witness. Not least because it hadn't escaped anyone that such a crowd would have been a painfully simple target for a terrorist. The march began at the Place de la République, where Parisians stood shoulder to shoulder and filled the enormous square. They held banners calling for peace, they sang the national anthem, they held hands. Reporting on the march, I was looking for a vantage point from which to take a photo. I worked my way through the throng to the middle of the square and climbed up onto the stone balustrades by the Metro entrance. It was only then, standing on the metre-high balustrade, that I got a perspective of the scale of the march. The wide boulevards stretching from every corner of République were all flooded with people. As far as the eye could see, there were Parisians who were declaring resistance against terror. They say 2 million people marched and the president at the time, Francois Hollande, said that Paris was the capital of the world that day.

Yes, this was Paris. These were its people. And they were strong. It was a strange and historic time for the Parisians. And it was a strange way to start a new life for me, standing on that stone railing and trying to understand it all. Little did we know that within a year we'd be going through it again tenfold, when more terrorists struck multiple Parisian locations in one night, killing 130 people. But this gathering was my first real look at the City of Paris and its people.

Even now, when I walk across République I look at those stone balustrades and think back to my first days in Paris. I think back to how admirable the Parisians all seemed to me that day. And I think about how much I had wanted to be part of it all.

1.2 The perfect apartment

When the coverage of the attack began to wind down, it was time for me to move out of my hotel and into an apartment. I flew back to Sweden to gather the rest of my belongings and to figure out where I'd live in Paris. What many people don't realize is that apartment hunting in Paris is like searching for wild truffles. Sure, you can find them. You can even find excellent ones if you're extremely lucky. But one thing is for sure, you need a lot of luck to even find a bad one. As it turned out, I didn't learn this lesson for several years because I was among the lucky ones. The perfect apartment landed in my lap before I had even started looking.

It came in the form of an email from a Parisian woman. She had also spent the past few years in Stockholm and when she heard I was moving to Paris, she had offered to help. I responded that the only thing I needed was an apartment. On a snowy January afternoon as I was set to leave Sweden for good, my inbox pinged with good news.

I think I've found an apartment for you. It's typically Parisian, on the seventh floor and under the roofs. It's right in the middle of Paris, a perfect location, and the view is beautiful. You can see the Centre Pompidou from the window.

I had no idea that the Centre Pompidou was a modern art museum. I certainly didn't know that Monsieur Pompidou was once the President of France either. I'd figure all that out later. The email continued:

There are two rooms and it has a bed, a fully equipped kitchen, a big working table, a bathtub, a washing machine, and a couch. It's 750 euros a month.

This sounded too good to be true. There had to be a catch.

The only thing is the size. It's 20 metres squared. Don't ask me how they fit everything there. It's the magic of Paris. But you know, living under the roofs of Paris is part of the experience. You'll feel like a poet or painter.

PS: there's no elevator either.

Ah, well there's the catch, I thought. It's tiny and there's no elevator. But how bad could seven flights of stairs be? And how small was 20 square metres (or 215 square feet, for that matter)? And what was a

Pompidou? More importantly, who cared? A few moments later, she'd forwarded me a few photos of the tiny apartment. The picture I liked the most was the view from the bedroom window. Hundreds of silver metal rooftops and red chimney pots stretched off to the horizon. *Les toits de Paris*, as Parisians call them, the rooftops that had inspired thousands before me and would inspire thousands more. The picture was incredible. What fortune to have a top-floor apartment in Paris with a view.

I said I'd take the place before I'd even visited. The landlady sent me the details and the address: 48 rue Greneta, 75002. Now, that address probably means as little to you as it did to me, so imagine my surprise when I typed it into Google Maps and found it was in the dead centre of Paris. Yes, if Paris was a dartboard - and the city limits do indeed form a big circle - then my new address was the bullseye. I pored over the online map as my excitement built, learning that I was to live just seconds from the famed market street rue Montorgueil and the pedestrianized zone of the second arrondissement. They were just words on the map to me at that point. In fact, I had no idea that an arrondissement was a district, nor that there were 20 that spiralled out across the city like a snail shell. And I didn't really care.

Instead, I took a virtual stroll down rue Greneta on Google Street View. It was narrow, paved with cobblestones, and full of little shops. It looked so charming, so old, so intriguing. I clicked from one end of the street to the other. Even the cobblestones were eye-catching, arranged in mesmerizing wavy lines. I researched the street online and found it was around 800 years old. 800 years old! Imagine!

And what's this?! The French author Honoré de Balzac had even described the street in an 1837 novel. But he seemed less impressed. He wrote that it was: "... a street where all the houses, crowded with trades of every kind, have a repulsive aspect. The buildings are horrible. The vile uncleanliness of manufactories is their leading feature..."

By God, I'd gone too far. I snapped my laptop shut and hoped that Balzac was wrong. Surely Paris had cleaned up its act over the past few centuries, right? I finished packing my bags and headed to Paris to find out for myself; this time on a one-way ticket.

1.3 Moving to Paris

A lot of people who move to Paris do it with a fixed time plan. You often hear expats saying "I'm here for six months" or, for those who've stayed on, "I was only supposed to be here for a month". But it was never like that for me. I booked a one-way ticket to Paris and that was it. I'd spent the previous four years in Sweden, but that chapter was over: I had nothing and no one to stay for. Armed with a British passport from my English mum, I could essentially live and work anywhere in Europe. Australia, where I was born and raised, seemed like a distant memory and was inconveniently located on the wrong side of the world. I wanted to be in Europe. Europe was exciting, exotic, fascinating. It seemed to me to be the pulse of the universe, and I wanted to have my finger firmly pressed on it. And why Paris? Well, why not, really? I'd grown up hearing my Dad's tales of a summer he'd spent on a *péniche* on the Seine River. His Dad before him had similar jaunts in Paris too. As for me, I'd half-heartedly studied French at university and now seemed as good a time as any to put my skills into practice.

I also figured there was more to Europe than just Sweden, of course, and it was time to move on after four years. But I felt a tinge of regret leaving, as it seemed I'd made a name for myself in my last week in Sweden. I'd been in the far north of the country filming a YouTube video about the unusual way some Swedes say the word *yes*. Instead of saying "ja" (pronounced 'yah') like the rest of the Swedes, they do a sharp intake of breath as if they were shocked or surprised. We made a 90-second video where I walked around asking locals about this bamboozling sound. It turned out it wasn't just me who found it amusing. The video went viral on YouTube. It had millions of hits in just days, and the story made headlines around the world. On the day I left Sweden, our little story was on the front cover of the biggest newspapers in the country. We'd tapped into something - a little language oddity - and people around the globe were curious about it. Sure, it was a silly story, but it made a big splash, and it seemed like a fitting bookend to my time in Sweden. As I boarded the flight for Paris, I was getting messages from Swedish media for my thoughts on this strange phenomenon. But I had to say no (as much as I'd have liked to have given a sharp intake of breath, instead). Yes, I was getting on a flight to Paris, a one-way flight, and it was time to move on to the next challenge. There'd be no radio or TV interviews because I wasn't looking back. And there was no way to do a call from the flight either, so it was impossible anyway. Of course, I felt a regret too. When anything goes viral like that, there's often a ripple effect that you can potentially surf into the sunset. But there was no way I could ride that particular wave in France: I'd have to try and start new ones.

Yes, I was leaving Sweden and perhaps I'd never come back. That's what I thought. How wrong I was. But that's for later in the book.

I arrived in Paris for good in late January, 2015. My first week in Paris didn't seem real. I was so focused on the Charlie Hebdo attack that I didn't stop to think. But now it was different. I got off the plane at the Charles de Gaulle airport and I was hungry. Hungry for the food, the language, the people. Hungry to figure out France, and whether Paris was as incredible as everyone seemed to think. And I was curious to investigate the culture, observe the idiosyncrasies of the French, and marvel at the oddities of their language.

But, as I strode through the arrival hall at the Charles de Gaulle airport, all I could think of was the telephone booths. Real, old-fashioned phone boxes. The kind I hadn't seen in years, the kind that had been stripped from the streets of tech-savvy Sweden long ago. Stockholm is so advanced that even the homeless people accept payments by credit card (seriously). But in Paris there were still functional phone booths at the international airport. I don't know why it made such an impression on me, but those phone boxes stuck in my mind. I suppose it kind of felt like I was stepping back in time. I surveyed the rest of the grotty and unimpressive airport, which is regularly ranked among the worst in the world. And I thought, how on earth can a world capital like Paris be giving its visitors such a lacklustre first impression? I splurged on a taxi to my new home, understanding now why a friend in Sweden had warned me to take cash - the taxi drivers didn't accept card payments. And mine didn't seem to accept the use of online maps either: he got us lost while trying to use a map book to navigate central Paris. Was he hustling me? Was he taking me the long way? At the time, I didn't know where we were going either - I didn't have any internet on my phone - and I was no savvier than any of the thousands of tourists taking similar trips each day.

The cab driver pulled up on my new street, rue Greneta, and parked on the kerb outside my new front door. Immediately, all my concerns about "old-fashioned Paris" were dashed away when I took in that entrance. I was gobsmacked. What a doorway! The kind of doorway that might make a Paris Instagrammer stop in their tracks. It was enormous, wide and tall enough to let through horses and carriages once upon a time. The double doors were set in an impressive stone archway that stretched up to the top of the next floor. The door had an inbuilt window, behind which the *gardienne* (building manager) lived. The wooden doors looked far too heavy to open, but a closer inspection revealed a normal-sized door hidden within. To the side of the doors were mysterious stone ornaments that I'd later learn were in place to stop wagon wheels from damaging the frame. I stood there gaping at the building as the taxi driver pulled away. And just as my jaw finally closed, it was set to drop again. The landlady, a young French woman, opened the door and revealed the courtyard.

As lovely as the Frenchwoman was (and she was indeed a lovely Frenchwoman), it was the courtyard that stopped me in my tracks for the second time in a row. It looked like a rainforest. The alleyway, paved with huge, uneven cobblestones, was open to the early evening skies above. It was lined on both sides with a wild array of greenery, trees several metres tall, and the windowsills on each side were crowded with plants and vines. And there at the end of the alley, stretching seven floors high, was the building I was to call home for the next two years.

The landlady pointed to the sloping grey roof at the top, which had two windows facing in our direction, and said it was my apartment. She looked me up and down. I had a suitcase in each hand, my whole life.

"Is that all?" she asked, in English, thank God. I nodded. "You know there's no elevator, right?"

Yep, I smiled, and lifted both suitcases in one go. We crossed the courtyard and got to the winding, polished wooden staircase. The landlady hit the stairs with gusto, leaving me lagging behind with my heavy luggage. And I can tell you, even with the adrenaline that was pumping through my veins from this new chapter in my life, I didn't make it up the stairs without a few pit stops. Who'd have thought climbing seven flights of stairs could be such a chore?

But when I finally made it to the top, where the landlady was waiting for me with an open door, my weary arms and tired legs were soon a distant memory. I stepped into the apartment; and while it was tiny and bare, it was also incredible.

The front door led into a living room with a sofa and a surprisingly big desk by a narrow window. It looked over Paris to the west. Behind a curtain was a separate kitchen, minuscule, but with a fridge, a sink, a stove plate, and big windows facing the north.

"Look, that's Sacré-Coeur in the distance," the landlady said, pointing towards Montmartre across the rooftops. "Not a bad view for while you're making your morning coffee, *non*?"

The sun was setting and I watched as the lights flicked on across the city.

"Not bad at all," I responded, amazed that I could count the sight of such a monument among my daily views.

She continued the tour, leading me into the bedroom. It too was tiny, but arranged in such a way to make it seem spacious. The bed was a futon, positioned under the slant of the ceiling. Above the bed was another window, and the woman heaved it open, a tricky task considering it was built into the sloping roof. This meant you had to lift the whole weight of the window, then use the latch to prop it open. But the effort was worth it - Paris to the south stretched out before me in the crisp January evening, and it was glorious. Our building appeared to be a little higher than all the other ones, so we had a bird's eye view of the city. And thanks to the long tree-lined courtyard below us, there was a good distance before the nearest block of flats, which was much smaller than ours. All this added a superb effect of openness, perhaps a trick of depth perception; meaning it felt like we were outside of Paris and looking in on it. And the rooftops - of which we could see hundreds - were a beautiful mix of grey zinc sheeting and terracotta tiles, adorned with the same red chimney pots, and laid out all higgledy piggledy to the horizon. I'd already seen this view, of course. It was the one from the photo. But that picture hadn't done it justice. I could see for miles. The fresh air was a little too fresh for the landlady, who closed the window and brought me back to reality.

The tour wasn't finished. Partly hidden by some big wooden saloon doors was my new bathroom, complete with a bath (also under the slanted roof), a handheld shower head, and a sink. Behind another closed door was a toilet. By my count, this was a five-room apartment. The magic of Paris indeed.

"This seems a lot bigger than 20 metres squared," I said.

"*Oui*, they don't include the space under the slanted ceiling," she responded. "So technically, your whole bed is in a kind of negative space. It isn't counted. Neither is the bathroom."

She explained to me that most apartment blocks in Paris had tiny rooms like this on the top floor. They're called "*chambres de bonnes*", or maid's quarters, and were once homes for the servants of the wealthier residents below. Now they're mostly used by students or people looking to save a few euros on accommodation. So, for a young man like me who was keen to live centrally, it made perfect sense to be living in a *chambre de bonne*.

I was learning so much, but as pleasant as the conversation was, it wasn't long before I got my first taste of French admin.

"*Alors*, we have to go through the condition of everything in the apartment," said the landlady.

Sure, I agreed, that sounded reasonable. What I didn't realize was that she literally meant we had to go through *everything*. Everything! We spent the next hour walking around the apartment and checking the condition of every wall, window, and piece of furniture. We both had to write *bon état* ("in good condition") as every last item in the home was reviewed. If there was a scratch on the wall or a crack in the window we had to both write "mauvais état". I thought it was a joke. I suggested we simply agree on the things that *weren't* in good condition, but that didn't fly.

"*Non*, this is just how we do it in France," she shrugged.

Turns out I'd be hearing that one again, and again, and again during my first months in Paris. The French have their own way of doing things, and if that involves plenty of paperwork, then all the better. The apartment papers were just the same: two full copies, handwritten, and meticulously cross checked. When the documents were all finally signed, there was a mood shift and the landlady brightened up. We got to chatting again. She explained that her parents had used the apartment as a backup home, but had taken to renting it out in recent years. She told me that every tenant so far had been Japanese, all of whom had liked the practical use of space. She said, with a worried smile, that I was by far the tallest tenant, too, adding that she hoped I didn't find it too small. I'm six foot three, and she had gauged it pretty well. The apartment was way too small for me. Especially the shower, which I ended up using while in a Gollum-like crouch.

She glanced at her watch, noticed that the evening had truly set in, and said it was time for her to leave. She handed over the keys.

"One piece of advice," she said from the doorway. "This place gets freezing cold in winter and boiling hot in the summer. You're right under the rooftops, so there's not much you can do to fight the elements. Just use some extra blankets in the winter and get a fan for summer. It's like that with all the *chambres de bonnes*… you'll get used to it. Oh, and you'll get used to the stairs too. It gets easier after a while."

She went to shut the door.

"Oh, and I forgot to mention. There's a communal toilet just outside of your door, but no one uses it. Most apartments have their own toilets nowadays, including yours. But check it out when you have a second, you can see the Eiffel Tower from the window."

I played it cool and smiled as we said our *au revoirs*. But as soon as I heard her footsteps fade down the stairs, I threw open the front door, rushed into the tiny bathroom, stretched myself over the toilet and pressed my face up against the window. And as promised, there she was. The Iron Lady, La Tour Eiffel - granted, quite far away - but right outside my window, with nothing blocking the view. Before I even had time to take it all in, the tower lit up in sparkling lights, as it does for the first five minutes of every evening hour. I suppose it would have been quite a romantic moment, but I was all alone. And I was leaning over a particularly unkempt communal toilet. But I was in Paris and I could feel the magic in the air.

1.4 Rue Montorgueil

Rue Montorgueil is among the best streets in Paris and the hardest one to spell. Right from the beginning, I thought it was the epitome of Paris. The road was lively in the morning as the fishmongers and grocers set up their stalls. The cafe terraces were crowded during the day and the bars were buzzing at night. It was unique, it was interesting, and it was a stone's throw from my front door. I spent those first few weeks much like a nervous tourist might. I often looked into the restaurants, but felt too self-conscious to take up a full table to myself. I picked a few spots that seemed to work for lone diners and favoured them to begin with. I still wasn't even remotely confident speaking French and I ended up eating a lot of takeaway food.

But while I didn't like eating alone, I had no problems exploring alone. Rue Montorgueil was fantastic itself, but the whole *quartier* was rich in history that was in plain sight and still unfolding each day. Not long after I moved into the area, renovation workers found several mass graves under the local Monoprix supermarket. They uncovered the skeletons of 200 people, presumably the victims of a disease or catastrophe. After all, the supermarket was built on the site of a 13th century hospital. But what was strangest of all for me was how no one seemed to care. The supermarket didn't even close down, and Parisians continued their daily shopping while archaeologists excavated the site below. My own street had once housed an 800-year-old hospital. And likely there had been buildings there before it, maybe twice as old. And there I was, an Australian man in his twenties, trying to make sense of it all.

Flanking the supermarket, at the eastern end of rue Greneta was rue Saint-Denis, a road that stretched from the river Seine towards Montmartre. The street bisected mine amid a handful of sex shops, which sold porn DVDs with dusty covers, and all manner of sex toys. But I didn't know this at the time - if I was too nervous to walk into a restaurant, you can bet your last euro that I wasn't browsing around in sex shops. I checked them out much later in a drunken and giggly haze with the woman who'd one day become my wife. But I'm getting ahead of myself again. The sex shops were hard to miss: they were lit up in garish neon, often with ageing strippers on the doorstep, smoking cigarettes and beckoning to the passersby. Or maybe they were prostitutes. Hell, maybe they were neither. I never stopped to find out. But those neon lights caught my attention. There was nothing like this in Sweden, and absolutely not in the part of Australia where I'd grown up either. I felt like I was at the centre of the universe.

And if all this wasn't enough, the district boasted exquisite covered passages from the 19th century, built so Parisians could go shopping without getting their feet muddy. The closest one to me was the remarkable Passage du Grand Cerf, built in 1825. Its glass ceiling three floors above let the sun sparkle down onto a curious collection of shops selling everything from jewellery to antique furniture. This was the kind of elegant attraction that people crossed the world to see - and for me it was just a shortcut to the Metro.

Yes, it was safe to say that I loved my new *quartier*, but not everything was running as smoothly back at the apartment. Several weeks into my stay I still had no internet. I had bought a new internet box, but it didn't work. And I found out pretty quickly that the only thing harder than living without internet in France is trying to get internet installed in Paris. Getting online was the first of my many bang-your-head-against-the-wall forays into getting anything done in France. And it wasn't a problem limited to just my apartment. On one of those early days, when ducking out to the shops, I met my neighbour on the top floor for the first time. He was a young guy, curly brown hair, and was smoking a cigarette by the communal window at the top of the stairs.

"*Salut, mec,*" he said with a broad grin.

I'd never heard the word *mec* before but I didn't want to betray my lack of French know-how this early in the relationship. He introduced himself as Stephane, a student who'd come to Paris from the city of Grenoble in the French Alps, and he had just moved in too. He asked if I'd managed to get internet up here on the top floor. I told him I hadn't, but must have said so in such diabolical French that he decided we'd continue in English.

"I also 'ave no weefee, wino," he said. I figured *weefee* meant wifi, but it would be months before I figured what he meant by *wino*. "But eef *you* get weefee, maybe you geev me your weefee password and we share?" he said with a wink.

"Sure," I said.

"*Ah, merci,*" he said, putting out his cigarette in an ashtray that apparently lived on the corridor's windowsill. He turned to leave. "*A plus, mec.*"

A few thoughts were going through my head as I walked down the 118 stairs (I'd counted them by now). First, why did he keep calling me *mec*, and what did it mean? Second, it was clear that both Stephane and I were rubbish at each other's language. Perhaps we could teach each other, I thought. And third, how was I going to solve this blasted internet problem?

1.5 The raw bacon

Unlike the Stockholm headquarters, our Paris office in the 19th arrondissement was very petite indeed. It was just a startup at this point, with only one other employee, the British editor who considered it his duty to Frenchify me as quickly as possible.

"You look like a Swede, mate, what's going on with that haircut? What's that jacket? You're in old Europe now," he told me when we first met in January. "And have you got a French girlfriend yet? It's part of the contract, you know?"

The editor wasn't thrilled by my lack of French and figured a French girlfriend would be the quickest fix. But there weren't any French girls in our office (and our office had no space for them, anyway). We worked in a room with glass walls, boxed off from an architecture firm that occupied the whole floor. As I walked to my desk each morning, the architects would raise an eyebrow and examine me. These architects would turn out to be my main source of understanding the French in those early days. But from the beginning, they were the ones who were observing me, as if I were some Australian lizard, trapped from 9 to 6 every day in their glass terrarium. And they didn't seem pleased with their catch either. Their first complaint against me came within days of my starting the job, and my editor was the messenger.

"Did you eat lunch in the reception area yesterday?" he asked me.

"Uh, yeah I think I did. They were all eating in the kitchen, there was no space, so I just ate on the go on one of the seats."

"Right, well there's been a complaint. The receptionist wants it to be known that the reception area is for welcoming people, not for eating lunch. They're a particular bunch, mate, watch your step."

"But… why didn't she just tell me at the time?" I asked.

"No idea, just keep an eye out. And the French never eat 'on the go' anyway."

Wow. What a minefield. And what an unfair minefield. How can you avoid breaking the sacred French lunchtime codes if you don't know what they are? To make matters worse, I was still feeling self-conscious. I didn't dare to plonk myself down at the lunchtime table with the architects for their daily wine-filled feasts. I hated that I didn't speak good French, and I found it embarrassing that I wouldn't understand a conversation. Not least because I was working in a job where I should be able to communicate in French. I felt like an imposter. The competence in French would come, of course, but in those early days it seemed impossible. So as far as lunch was concerned, I decided if I *was* going to eat in the office, I'd do it surreptitiously at my desk. But of course that led to another of my downfalls.

One day, I went to the local supermarket to grab some cheese, bread, and ham. I bought plenty of it and made a few sandwiches in a hurry in the kitchen to avoid the architects. I smuggled my loot into the office and wolfed the sandwiches down before anyone spotted me. You see, lunch for me has never been much more than a necessity. Sure, I enjoy a good meal as much as the next man, but a sandwich would suffice for lunch on a work day. And where I'm from, it's not wildly unusual to eat at your desk. So that's simply what I did. I told the editor that there was plenty of leftover ham and bread if he fancied some.

About an hour later he came back from the kitchen.

"Mate, did you say there was leftover ham? I couldn't find it."

I headed to the kitchen fridge with him. Had the architects taken my ham? Surely, surely they hadn't eaten my ham. But would I finally have a one-up on them?

"There it is," I said, grabbing the ham from the fridge.

The editor raised an eyebrow.

"Mate, that's not ham... that's bacon. That's raw bacon. Did you cook it before you ate it."

"Uh, no. Shit. I made it and ate it so quickly..." There was a long pause. "What happens if you eat raw bacon?"

Yes, I had eaten raw bacon and didn't even notice. Perhaps it was the rush of the smuggle. Perhaps it was the shame of sneaking my own lunch into an office to eat in secret. Perhaps it was the fact that I have a terrible sense of taste in general. Or perhaps, the editor said, after we had searched online for whether eating raw bacon will kill you, perhaps it was something worse. When the dust had settled and it was decided I wouldn't die, the editor asked me the question I'd been dreading.

"Mate, you know it said pretty clearly on the packet that it was raw bacon... Now tell me, and tell me honestly... just how bad is your French?"

The answer was obvious. My French was abysmal. We agreed that if I was to be carrying out even halfway decent interviews with French people, I'd need to improve my language skills. I'd promised the bosses that I'd pick French up quickly and while I *had* studied it ten years earlier, relearning it wasn't going to happen overnight. The editor suggested a refresher course and I signed up that evening. As much as I didn't want to go back to French class, I figured that at least I could meet some new people. But the classes didn't start for a while, so I'd have to experiment with other ways to learn. I'd been living in France for about a month and didn't have any friends, French or otherwise. So in a country full of French people... just how are you supposed to meet them, I wondered. The answer, it turned out, was just around the corner.

1.6 The 'guys'

The French have a great word for a person who likes to wander about aimlessly; that person is a *flâneur* (or a *flâneuse* if you're female). But before I knew the word, I knew the idea, because that's exactly what I was in those early days. A flâneur. I rarely knew what I was looking at, or where I was exactly, and I certainly didn't have any context, but I loved it anyway.

Working in an office from Monday to Friday during a Paris winter meant I had no daylight hours to explore the city, except during the tourist-packed weekends. Those first weeks and months I spent in Paris must have been what it was like for tourists in the old days. I had no internet, no plans, no ideas… I just walked and walked and walked.

One Saturday morning I was on the right bank of the Seine River, in an area I'd later learn was called the Marais. The houses were all built on top of each other, with no room to breathe, but it wasn't claustrophobic. At least, I didn't think so. I thought it was intoxicating and exciting. I felt I could pass through a passageway, or a doorway, or a courtyard, and find a hidden treasure. And that's exactly what happened. One day I was exploring the Village Saint Paul, a small collection of boutique shops, hotels, and restaurants, when a doorway opened onto the most stunning outdoor basketball court I've ever seen. Despite the cold, a bunch of locals were playing an intense game of streetball. But even though I was a basketballer myself, that's not what caught my attention. It was the setting.

Looming ominously and impressively over the north end of the court was the Eglise Saint-Paul-Saint-Louis. Because most of the buildings in central Paris are six or seven floors high, churches like this one often seem even more gargantuan. The court itself was flanked by a stone wall, the longest surviving stretch of the city wall that encircled

Paris 800 years ago. It was built by King Philippe Auguste and was the envy of Europe at the time. Years later I'd develop a fascination with this wall, track down its vestiges, and plot its course among the buildings that had swallowed it up over the centuries. But on that day, I just liked the look of it, and I watched the basketballers sitting with their backs against it. Further along, children were kicking balls to each other, bouncing them off the ancient stones. Eventually I turned my attention to the court. And I was overcome by the need to be part of the game.

The next day, I arrived at the courts again, this time ready to play. But, with my limited French that made me too nervous to walk into a restaurant, imagine how tough I found it to ask if I could play. It might sound silly, but summoning the courage to join in was one of the more difficult things I've done in my life. Now, this might not sound all that tricky, especially if you're a happy-go-lucky child reading this. But as an adult in a foreign country, not understanding how the rules worked, I found it to be very challenging. Let me put this into context. I've played basketball for my entire life. I know the rules inside out. I know many variants of how to play streetball, and I even realize how the rules can change slightly from country to country. But even though basketball is a subject I could call myself an expert on, I was still nervous about joining the game. This is what it's like to start a new life in a new setting, especially in Paris. Sure, you may know how to order a beer in a bar, or park a car, or bring a gift to someone on their birthday. But when you're not sure how to do something in another language, your mind can play tricks on you.

So there I was, just like a child again. Just like a boy, standing in front of some other boys, about to ask if I could play. And I was riddled with fear. I picked my target, a guy standing with his back to the ancient city wall and watching the game. I started in French, and asked him a vague question about how it all worked.

"*Comment ça marche ici?*" I said, or something to that effect.

Honestly, I probably said something more like "How it work for to play basketball with us in here today?" I guess that's how it sounded to him, anyway, because he answered in English. Perfect English, would you believe it? It turned out he was a Parisian who taught English to high schoolers. He decided to take me under his wing and explained that it was pretty straightforward. You make a team of four, wait for a game to finish, then challenge the winning team. All you really had to do was make it known that you were up next. With that, he said I could play on his team, then yelled out something to the guys who were mid-game.

"*Les gars, on a la prochaine.*"

My existing knowledge of French, and of course the context, was enough for me to know that he'd just announced we'd be playing the next game. But there was one bit that made no sense.

"What did you say to them at the start? *Laygar?* At least it sounded like *laygar?*"

"Oh, *les gars,*" he said with a chuckle. "Yeah, it's kind of funny, it just means *guys. Gar* is short for *garçon,* which means boy, but it's just another way to say dude, mate, or *mec.*"

Ah, so *mec* means dude, I thought. That's what the neighbour, Stephane, had called me. But the "les gars" bit still didn't make sense to me.

"So, why did you say '*les gars*'? Surely that means 'the guys', no?"

"Ah, you've got a long way to go, my friend. You're not going to learn this language if you expect logical explanations. The best way is to repeat everything. Like a parrot. Why do we say 'hello the guys'?

Why do we think half our nouns are masculine and half are feminine? I don't know. But everyone does it, and you should too."

"Thanks, *mec*," I said, deciding that I'd adopt my first bit of French slang.

How lucky to have stumbled upon a language teacher to guide me through my first basketball experience. I had no idea at the time, but 'the guys' I'd meet on this basketball court would become like a Paris family for me - and a huge source of learning about French people, their language, and especially their slang. Yes, I was lucky and I was ready to shoot some hoops. There was a whole world in front of me and I was ready to jump into it. And just like that, the game being played was over and it was our turn to step onto the court.

Game on, *les gars*.

1.7 Another email

Belleville is one of those parts of Paris with a wonderful name. It literally means "Beautiful Town" but it's the sound of the name that I like the most. Say it out loud, it kind of sounds like a very sexy "bell veal". Belleville. Belleville. Belleville. I like the way your tongue presses twice against the back of your top teeth when you say it, I like those rolling elles. Unfortunately, the place isn't anywhere near as beautiful as the name. But that will change: it's quickly developing and will probably be the trendiest part of town soon. Heck, maybe it is already by the time you're reading this. Paris doesn't mess around when creating trendy neighbourhoods.

Anyway, the reason I was sitting in my apartment repeating the word Belleville in a sexy accent was because one afternoon I'd got another email that would eventually change my life. This time it was from a Swedish woman named Lina who I'd met at a party in Stockholm.

Hej, I've just moved to Paris for six months of study and I don't know anyone here, so if you wanna grab a drink, I'm in Belleville.

Unfortunately the Swedes don't pronounce Belleville in a sexy way. They go overboard with the elles and make it fun and silly like an ABBA song. But I wasn't complaining. I'd never been to Belleville; I was alone in Paris; and I couldn't think of a better way to spend an evening than having a drink in Beautiful Town with a beautiful Swedish woman.

So I met her one winter night and we walked through the Buttes-Chaumont park, which is the closest thing Paris has to an Indiana Jones movie set. Afterward, we stopped for a drink in a dive bar. I told her about my neighbour and my internet problems. She said her apartment smelled like cigarettes. I confessed about the raw bacon and she told me how she had locked her laundry inside a laundromat in Belleville. She was getting it all wrong too, and it was nice to be able to laugh it off with someone in the same boat. We were two strangers in a strange land and we planned to meet again that Saturday night.

It's impossible to remember which of us chose Saturday night, and whether that person knew that it was Valentine's Day. But to hell with it now, it was a great move if it was on purpose. Or a fortunate accident. We were both single. Why not spend Valentine's Day together, we reasoned. It was a date, why not? And what better city for Valentine's Day than Paris? But how to do it? And considering I'd just paid the two-month deposit on my new place, how could I do it cheaply? Surely, surely it was easy to be romantic on a budget in Paris. Then again, how romantic do you want to get on a second date? Or was it a first date?

We decided to spend the evening taking a stroll to the Eiffel Tower. Neither of us had been there after sunset, and we were keen to see it up close for the hourly light show, the blinding sparkles, which I'd only ever seen from my toilet. Along the way, we stopped at a supermarket and grabbed a bottle of cheap champagne and some *charcuterie* cold meat, then headed for the tower. In those days, you could walk straight off the street and directly underneath it. After the attacks in November later that year, the city installed a glass wall that made it impossible to enter without going through security checks. But back then, on Valentine's Day in 2015, there were no gates, no fences, no queues. It was still wide open, beautiful, and carefree. It was my first time visiting the tower as a resident of Paris and I loved it. I'd later learn that many Parisians have never climbed it and didn't care for it, but I didn't feel that way. I thought it was breathtaking.

We walked beneath the tower, stared shamelessly up under her iron skirt, then moved on to the Champ de Mars park, where the air was filled with the popping of champagne bottles. It wasn't until I opened our own that I realized we had forgotten to bring anything to drink it from. "No matter," she said, and took a swig straight from the bottle.

"I can appreciate the finer things in life, but I'm not against taking a good swig from a cheap bottle of champagne," she said. Or something like that.

Of course, I don't remember *exactly* what she said, because I was thinking, "Wow, what a gal. The kind of gal who'd go out with a guy like me, and not care that I'd bought the cheap bottle without any cups or glasses."

My thoughts were interrupted by a collective gasp from the crowd as the tower erupted into the hourly light show. Thousands of light bulbs all over the tower flashed and sparkled furiously, brilliantly, and romantically. Lina huddled closer to me and we watched until the sparkling died out.

We eventually decided to head back to the city on foot, and strolled along the Seine until we reached rue de Rivoli in the fancy first arrondissement. A welcoming and surprisingly cheap-looking bar caught my attention. We went in and ordered a pair of gin and tonics as a nightcap. The drinks were cheap, which was perfect for a broke journalist and a student. The waiters were lovely, perhaps caught up in the romance of the night, or perhaps looking for a tip from two tipsy foreigners. Who knows? But what I do know is that they got chatting with us and seemed infected by our good mood. As we went to leave, the bartender produced two shots of liqueur from nowhere and insisted they were on the house.

"Welcome to Paris, I can see a great future for you two," he said with a smile.

And a waitress handed each of us a red rose.

"*Oui*, Happy Valentine's Day to you both," she added.

We took the shot, said thank you, and headed into the streets once again, positively intoxicated by the romance in the air. Or perhaps it was the liqueur. In fact, it was almost certainly the liqueur. Because that's the only way I can explain my next ill-conceived idea.

We walked along the covered footpath of the rue de Rivoli, heading eastwards, past all the designer stores and luxury hotels. And then I was blinded. My eyes were hit by the sheer beauty of a hotel lobby. It was so luxurious, so opulent. I had to know more.

"Come on, let's see what's inside. Pretend you own the place," I told Lina.

The interior was even more dazzling. It was almost *too* impressive. Like the sun, I couldn't quite look at it directly, and I let myself be drawn inside. A staff member walked past me carrying a silver tray, the chandeliers in the lobby reflected off the grand piano; we walked into the bar as if in a trance. It would have been a crime if we didn't take a closer look, wouldn't it? In fact, it would have been a crime if we didn't sit down and have at least one drink, no?

We sat at the bar. Another two gin and tonics were the order of the night, and it would be my treat, I insisted, oddly forgetting that we'd just been guzzling supermarket champagne from the bottle. We enjoyed the cocktails as the love-struck, drunken, hypnotized daze continued to carry us along.

When the glasses were empty, the bartender slid the receipt to me. Before I even saw the price, my eye was drawn to the two words at the top of the paper and I was snapped out of my dizzy haze. *Le Meurice*. Shit. Oh, shit! Were we at Le Meurice? One of the fanciest hotels in the entire country? Good lord, I thought, what surprise figure waits for me further down this piece of paper? I avoided looking at the price, and in mere milliseconds, I sobered up as I cast a furtive glance around the room. It was only then that I really took it all in. All of the other patrons were wearing black ties and suits. And were the staff members actually wearing gloves? And those low leather armchairs: they looked like they probably had lost items of jewellery between the cushions rather than loose change. *Bite the bullet*, I told myself. *Look at the bill.*

And so I did. And I wished I hadn't. Two gin and tonics. Two normal drinks. And they cost more than I'd pay for a month of groceries.

"You look pale," Lina said to me. "Are you alright?"

"Yes, I'm fine," I lied. "I think that liqueur went to my head, that's all."

"Shall we get a nightcap?" she asked.

"No!" I shouted, in panic. "No," I repeated, but this time more gently, coolly. "Let's go for a walk"

I paid for the drinks and we left the hotel. I didn't mention to Lina that it had been the most expensive round of drinks I'd ever paid for in my life. I just pretended I was the kind of journalist who typically popped into Le Meurice for a casual gin and tonic. Thank God we didn't get a room, I thought.

Before calling it a night, we headed back to the Seine for one last stroll along the river. We cut through the deserted courtyard of the Louvre, past the glass pyramids, and stopped at the Pont du Carrousel bridge. We laughed, we smiled, and we watched the barges glide by. I remember thinking how lucky I was to be standing with a woman like her. It was a perfect Paris moment.

That Valentine's Day still rates among the best nights I've had in my life. Cheap champagne, expensive gin and tonics, and the woman of my dreams on my arm. If you'd told me that in three years I'd be proposing to that same woman on that same bridge, I'd have believed it.

CHAPTER TWO

A roommate, language
lessons, fruit flies, and
terror in Paris.

2.1 Settling in

I made my first cheese and wine *faux pas* within the same hour. And
while it wasn't because of my terrible French, that was a factor. You
see, I'd figured that after a few months in France I'd have re-learned
French fluently. Or at least to a strong level. After all, I'd studied it at
high school and even university. Surely, it would all come flooding
back to me if I was surrounded by Parisians, ducking into boulangeries,
befriending the locals. But as it turned out, I was hardly advancing at
all. My colleague was British, my work was mostly translating French
into English, and I was spending a lot of my spare time with Lina, a
Swede. My priorities were way out of order, I decided. It was time to

concentrate on learning French. And since the French classes I'd signed up for were yet to begin, I had to take matters into my own hands.

After a few more encounters with Stephane, my neighbour from Grenoble, I suggested that we try to do a language exchange. The plan was that we'd each grab a bottle of wine, set a stopwatch for half an hour and then only speak French. When the alarm went off, we'd switch to English and we'd continue switching every 30 minutes until we ran out of wine. We organized our first class, and I offered to host it at my place. It'd be the first French guest I'd have at the apartment, and I was determined to make a good impression.

In an attempt to come across as a competent Parisian host, I'd gone to rue Montorgueil to grab some wine and cheese. I'd gotten that bit right; a good Parisian host would absolutely be prepared with cheese and wine for their guests, and they take great pride in doing it well.

But I got the wine bit wrong, to begin with. When I'd asked the shopkeeper for something cheap, he had shuddered, and reluctantly suggested a Bordeaux. It was even worse with the cheese, the buying of which is an art form in France. You're supposed to go into the shop, have a lengthy discussion with the *fromageur* about what's particularly tasty this season, explain what you plan to eat with the cheese, maybe taste a piece or two, pause and consider; then make your purchase and be on your way. I didn't know all this, of course. Cheese shops aren't even remotely common where I'm from in Australia. So, I walked in, surveyed the counter of cheeses, and asked for a mix.

"Certainly, *monsieur*, what would you like a mix of?"

"Well, your best hits, really. A bit of everything," I responded.

"Could I interest *monsieur* in our aged hard cheeses? This Comté is 18 months old."

"Sure. And with it, maybe just a little bit of this and that would be perfect," I said with a smile. Gosh, what a great customer I was! Not too fussy, happy to accept whatever was on offer.

I didn't realize it at the time, nor for a good while afterwards, that I was essentially offending the *fromageur*. He was offering me his best, and I wasn't even interested in listening. He seemed to give up.

"Perhaps *monsieur* would like our pre-packaged cheese mix?" he said, pointing to a dusty looking corner in the glass display.

I said that the mix of cheeses sounded perfect. He handed me a plastic box with what looked to me like an exciting variety of cheeses, all in different colours and shapes. Yellow cubes, orange slices, there were even some green bits in there. All pre-cut and ready to eat. Oh what a treat, how Stephane would be impressed with my wine from a wine shop and my cheese from a *fromagerie!* I took my haul home and set it up on the vintage suitcase that I'd balanced on a box, my dining table for the next two years.

He arrived right on time and broke into a grin immediately.

"Eet's time to learn Engleesh, *wino*," he said.

Again with the *wino*. What *could* he mean? I ignored it again.

"Stephane! Welcome! *Bienvenue*! Shall we start in English?" I said.

"OK, sure," he said, his eyes taking in the feast I'd laid out on the table. "But first, what the hell is that? Is that cheese? What are the green pieces? It looks like fruit salad," he said with a laugh. "And let me see that wine. Bordeaux? What is that, cat piss? Let's start with my bottle, it's a Côte du Rhône from near my hometown. And remind me to teach you how to buy cheese after I teach you how to speak French."

Of course, Stephane's English wasn't this good, but these were the points he made in a mixture of English, French, and gesticulations. *Wild* gesticulations when it came to the cat piss bottle of wine. And after the first 30 minutes of French, I can admit that my efforts at speaking his language were as bad as my cheese choosing.

But the language exchange was a handy way to learn, at least for me. Our rule was if you didn't know a word, you couldn't say it in your native language. I had to try to explain it in French (and Stephane had to explain it in English). Because when it comes to language learning, it's too easy to resort to just dropping in English words when you're lost. Or to say "Oh, how do you say this?" and so on. So we ruled that out from the beginning. And as excruciating as it was for both of us, we struggled through and got to know each other the hard way.

Stephane told me that he wanted to learn English so he could watch the new *Game of Thrones* episodes without having to wait for the local TV channels to dub them into French. He explained that he was studying finance and had dreams of moving to New York or London. He added that he didn't have a girlfriend but was on the lookout. I told him that I was a journalist who played basketball. He thought I was crazy to move to Paris when I was from Australia, a sentiment I'd hear countless times from other young French people over the years.

It was a pleasant treat to get to know my neighbour, even if he didn't have an appetite for my green cheese. By the time we reached the bottom of the second bottle, the cat-piss red wine I'd bought, it felt like we were both somehow fluent in each others' languages. And I suppose we were pretty drunk. He took his leave and staggered across the top floor corridor to his own *chambre de bonne* apartment.

"Zairs a new episode of Game of Thrones, I think I'm ready to understand eet, *wino*," he said.

As he shut the door, I figured it out. *Wino* had nothing to do with my taste (or bad taste) for wine, not at all. He was saying "right now", but instead of doing the unrolled English R, which can be tricky for French speakers, he was switching the R for a W. So *right now* became *wight now*, or *wino* in a Grenoble accent. I never understood why he said "right now" to punctuate so many of his English sentences. Maybe it was a "lost in translation" thing; maybe they say "*juste maintenant*" all the time in eastern France. Who knew? I certainly didn't, but I took it to be one of Stephane's charms. And anyway, I had other things to focus on, *wino*.

2.2 The admin

If you're thinking of moving to Paris, or anywhere in France, you must be prepared for administrative difficulties. Specifically, you must be ready for rejection. That's just how it is, you'll apply for something and you won't get it. And the reason will be ridiculous. There'll be a missing signature. Something won't be stamped. Your dog's dental records will be out of date. Who knows. But there will be something. And the number one, ultimate secret for beating the system is to expect failure and smile when it happens. It's the only way to go.

And you know what? It really works. When you expect that things will fail, then you don't mind when it all goes pear-shaped. It's like a Jedi mind trick. You almost end up leaving happier when you leave whatever office it is without having gotten what you needed. Because you *will* suffer failure: it's part of the process. I'm convinced French admin workers are relieved when there's a document missing and they get to send papers to another desk. I can sense their satisfaction.

And I learned all this pretty quickly.

One of the cruel ironies for a newcomer in France is that you have to do all the hardest admin at the beginning. You can't wait around to improve your French if you want to open a bank account or get a social security number. Nope, you have to do it immediately: and though it hurts, you've gotta rip it right off the wound, like a bandaid. A lot of expats move to France with their French loved one, making the journey infinitely smoother: but that wasn't my situation. I was single, clueless, and desperately unprepared for the pain that came with peeling that bandaid off gently.

When I opened my bank account, for example, I was once again reminded of how impressive Sweden was, compared to France. In Sweden, I waltzed into a bank, asked to open a new account, and had one in minutes. In France, I had to book a meeting, endure that meeting for over an hour, and then leave the bank with a pile of documents as thick as a short novel.

When I arrived, the banker took me into a little office and made me sign ten lengthy documents, once for him and once for myself. Yes, that's right, 20 signatures.

"This, *monsieur*, is for online banking. You want online banking, yes?" he said.

"Well, yes, please," I responded.

He printed off another few pages twice, one set for each of us.

"And monsieur would like a bank card, yes?"

"Yes, please. But do we really need all this paper?" I asked.

He shrugged.

"This is just how we do it in France," he said.

But if I thought the bank was bad, I was in for a *real* treat trying to set up my social security account. The fact that I can be quite unorganized with these matters didn't help. The first time I went into the social security offices, I went simply with the goal of finding out exactly what I needed, right from the horse's mouth. I took the afternoon off work for the occasion. When I arrived at 2 pm on a Thursday, a sign out the front informed me that the offices were closed Thursday afternoons. Of course.

The second time around, I came armed with the necessary documents. Some of the online forums I visited suggested that a translated birth certificate might not be necessary, so I chanced it that an English one was fine. But I was wrong, of course. I had to get an "international apostille" sticker on the back of my birth certificate - which meant that it was now an internationally-recognized document. Then I paid a ridiculous amount of money for an official translation of my birth certificate, which I still consider to be the easiest translation job in history. "Born here, named this". It was high school French at best. When I finally submitted it, they still didn't accept it because there was no official signature or translation on the back of my birth certificate, the side that had nothing besides the *apostille* sticker. The word *apostille* was French, for God's sake, but it wasn't translated, signed, or stamped, so I had to start all over again and head back to the official translator.

Sometimes it's almost enough to break your spirit, but that's why you have to laugh.

Despite my struggles, I did have a few early victories. One was when I limped into the town hall on crutches after a cycling accident. I exaggerated that limp and let my voice falter when I handed over my papers. I winced at the mere effort of signing something. And the woman took pity on me, and helped me.

But nothing compared to the magic of occasionally saying I was Australian. Once I went to the Town Hall of the second arrondissement to set myself up as a tax-paying journalist, rather than a tax-paying citizen, after I heard rumours that there would be added benefits. It was a complicated procedure that called for French language mastery far beyond my own talents.

There was a young man behind the desk, whose thick glasses made his eyes seem twice as big as he sized me up. I asked him if he spoke English.

"You know," he said in fluent, but heavily accented, English. "We're told we don't have to speak English with people - even if we can."

He looked across the room as if he were about to sell me drugs. As if he could get in trouble if he was caught speaking English with me.

"Where are you from? America? England?" he said.

When I said Australia his eyes went almost frighteningly wide behind those glasses. His dream was to visit Australia. He'd been looking into the one-year work visa that was popular among many young French people. He was going through all my papers as he talked, chattering away about kangaroos, Sydney, and famous Australians.

"Tell me," he said. "What do you think of us French people? People say we are arrogant and rude, and there is a bit of truth to that, I think."

With my mind clearly on the importance of his help, I answered that I didn't think the French were rude at all, which was actually true. I honestly think it's all one big misunderstanding that comes from language criss-crossing, cultural differences, and too many tourists. But I didn't get into it then.

We kept chatting, he seemingly oblivious to the fact that there was a long queue piling up outside his small office. He asked what kind of vegetables we grew in Australia, except he pronounced it veg-er-ter-bles - four syllables, which I realized I actually preferred. All the while, he was flipping through my documents, ticking boxes, and explaining how I could get journalistic tax deductions in the years to come. Finally, he said I was set up as a tax-paying reporter in France and that I'd be getting generous returns if all his work was approved.

"I'll come back with good news," he said, leaving the room with my papers.

And he did. All I had to do was go out of his office and ask the woman at the front to co-sign a few documents. I was amazed; I'd tackled the dreaded French taxman and it was actually a rather lovely experience. When I got to the lady at the front, I offered a friendly "Do you speak English?" with a strong hint of an Australian accent to see if my luck would continue.

"*Non*," she grunted. "*On est en France, on parle français.*" We are in France, we speak French here.

Ah. Well, you can't win them all, I suppose.

2.3 The neighbours

"It's part of your job contract to date a French woman," my editor repeated.

I made sure to peruse my contract, just to be sure, before I introduced him to Lina, who I'd been seeing a lot more. The editor was dismayed. He was convinced that the only way I'd ever understand France was with a Frenchwoman on my arm. He was probably right. There's no quicker way to learn a language than to be immersed in it. Weekend visits to the French in-laws. Whispering sweet French nothings in the bedroom. Watching as they manoeuver the ridiculous

French admin for you (if only!). Oh, the benefits were surely endless. But I had a Swedish woman instead, meaning I was doomed to improve my Swedish and forever languish in French language purgatory.

One spring morning, Lina had stayed at my apartment after I'd gone to work. She texted me with what she called good news and bad news. The good news was that she'd washed the sheets. The bad news was that she'd thrown my pillowcases out the seventh-floor window.

"I didn't mean to do it, I was shaking the sheets out the window and I didn't know the pillowcases were in there."

"So what happened to the pillowcases?" I asked.

"I can see them. They're on someone's sunroof seven floors down. But it's not our apartment block, it's next door, and I don't know whose door to knock on. I have an idea to get them back, but you'll have to help me."

Lina was waiting for me when I got home, armed with a big ball of string and a few pieces of metal.

"We'll *fish* them back up!" she said, with a half-crazed look in her eyes.

"*That's* the plan?" I said with a laugh. "You're going to try and hook them from the seventh floor?"

We spent the next two hours dangling 15 metres of string, weighed down with a few nuts and bolts, and trying to hook pillow-cases with bent pieces of wire. The feeling of pure elation to eventually hook each of them was surely greater than any fisherman at the Seine River had ever felt. If only we could have seen the faces of the Parisians below when they saw the white pillowcases being reeled upwards past their kitchen windows.

As it turned out, we'd hear from my neighbours quicker than we thought. My phone rang a few days later and a man introduced himself in English as "Andrew from downstairs".

"I got the note you left, so here I am, calling you back," he said.

I'd slipped a note under his door after noticing his doormat was in the design of the Union Jack, the British flag. On the note, I told him that I was on the top floor if he ever fancied meeting a neighbour.

"Great! If you're home now, come up for a drink," I said.

He knocked on my door ten minutes later and came inside, impressed by the view from the apartment, but not by the size of it. In Paris apartments the ceilings tend to get progressively lower the higher you get up the building. In other words, those on the first few floors typically have the highest ceilings, while the apartments at the top are cramped and tiny. You can see it for yourself if you look carefully at the outside of Paris buildings, there'll be a noticeable difference between the first and fifth floor, for example. You can often see it even more tangibly from the stairwell inside, where it takes fewer and fewer steps to get between floors. When these buildings were made, the wealthiest residents lived near the ground and left their servants and maids up the top.

Anyway, my no doubt wealthier neighbour asked how I liked the building, and I told him that it was all good, besides my lack of internet connection. Weeks after my initial complaints, the internet team had finally visited and decided it was the fault of the telephone company, which had apparently cut the wrong wire. After more weeks of nothing happening, the phone team came out to repair that wire, and now I was waiting for the internet team again.

"The French won't do anything unless you get angry," Andrew said, adding he'd lived in Paris for decades now and had seen it all before. "I can call them if you like."

"Be my guest," I said.

With that, he phoned the internet provider and when they started to make excuses he proceeded to let loose on them.

"What's the point of having this piece of shit internet box if there's no bloody internet on it? I may as well throw it out the window! What kind of company are you running that you give internet boxes but don't make sure they're connected? This is bullshit."

Yikes.

While he may have been firm - even aggressive, perhaps - on the telephone, he was a pleasant chap to be around, and the tough guy act seemed to work. After he hung up, he told me that the internet team would be around on Friday. Amazing. It was a valuable lesson: don't let yourself be walked over or you'll never get anything done.

As the evening wore on, my guest took one more look out the window and tried to pinpoint his apartment below.

"Ah, it's lovely to have a kitchen window that looks over Paris," he said. "And you know, sometimes you can see the most unusual things. Last week I could swear I saw someone's washing fall down past my window. Then hours later, I saw it fly back up again."

2.4 The fruit flies

It was summer in Paris, the air was crisp, the fruit was fresh, and I was about to annoy the architects again. I'd found that spending full days in front of the computer screen wasn't doing anything for my health.

My editor had no taste for long lunches or exercise breaks, so I decided to start bringing fresh fruit into the office. No harm in that, I figured. I'd bring in bananas, apples, peaches, and I'd place them in a fruit bowl in the middle of the room for the team - which was growing to include the occasional intern or two. It was a good plan, but it didn't always go smoothly. One week I bought too much fruit for us all to manage.

By the time Monday came around I got to work before anyone else in the office only to realize I'd left the bloody fruit on the desk over the weekend. The peaches had turned into rotten corpses and they were swarming with fruit flies. And I don't mean just a regular swarm. I mean a swarm of biblical proportions. I had only minutes before the architects started to arrive, and I panicked. I threw the peaches into my little bin, tied the plastic bag tight, then ran it into the kitchen and launched it into the main kitchen bin. Then I came back to our glass-walled office for damage control. Shit, there were still hundreds of fruit flies - what to do? I opened the windows and shooed them out. Some left, but most of them stayed. I wasn't getting anywhere. I waved my arms around, tried to swat them. Anything to hide the evidence that I'd been eating food in the office again. And I'm ashamed to admit it, but I murdered some of them too. Innocent fruit flies! But that's how frightened I was of the architects, frightened enough to kill defenseless insects in cold blood.

It wasn't long until the architects started to arrive. Still very wary of me at this point, some said hello. Others ignored me, as usual. At this point there were only a dozen fruit flies remaining, so I left them alone, realizing it was better than attracting attention trying to get rid of them. I felt I'd escaped, gotten away with the perfect crime.

I cracked on with the day's work, irritated that I was having a slow start on one of the rare occasions that the editor wasn't in the office. An hour or so into the morning I had well and truly forgotten about the fruit flies and was starting to feel the urge for a mid-morning cup of tea. I stood up from my desk and stretched, then turned to head for the kitchen. But before I'd taken one step, I saw them. The horror. The fruit flies, which had obviously been frightened away by my mad efforts to kill them, had by now figured it was safe to come out again. They had congregated in scores on the ceiling and all over the glass walls that separated me from the architects. Shit shit shit. But… what's this? None of the architects had noticed. I could fix this. It could be worse. Yes, it could be much worse, I thought.

I was right. And it was going to be.

I headed for the kitchen, playing cool, acting like there weren't around 200 flying insects in my office. The same office I'd allegedly let mice into, which is another story, and which also explains why the architects didn't like me. And then I saw it.

In the kitchen was a second swarm of fruit flies. Some idiot had taken rotten fruit and dumped it in the kitchen bin an hour ago. That idiot was me. But at least no one knew that. I felt like a child again, facing imminent trouble from the adults. In a blind panic I grabbed the kitchen bin bag and smuggled it out of the office and into the elevator, then out onto the streets where I dumped it in a city bin. I ran to a nearby shop and bought fly spray, then raced back to the kitchen. Then, as much as I hate to say it, I sprayed the fruit flies to death until they were dropping all over the kitchen table and floor. I did this all without the architects knowing. I couldn't let them couldn't know. I was already a terrible guest. I swept away the corpses of the fruit flies from the kitchen table and opened the windows to get rid of the smell of the fly spray. And miraculously, no architects came in during the entire slaughter.

Sure, there were a few left in the kitchen, but not enough to notice, I thought. So I moved back to my cubicle and spent the rest of the morning trying to get rid of the evidence. Like a lizard catching flies in a terrarium, I sneakily disposed of the remaining fruit flies in my little glass office one by one until there were none.

But fruit flies are apparently stubborn little buggers. The survivors in the kitchen turned out to be a mini swarm. The architects found the invasion at around lunch time, and were baffled as to where it came from. Where was the fruit, they wondered. No one could figure it out and I wasn't about to turn myself in. I'm ashamed to say it, but they were still killing the flies when I left the office that evening. And I never said a word. It marked the last time I brought fruit into the office, and our diet returned to English biscuits and the occasional French croissant.

2.5 The lessons

Speaking French on the phone makes me nervous. Especially having to do it in front of other French speakers. And this was an unavoidable part of my job as a journalist in Paris. Even though the editor was aware of my terrible French, he insisted that I make phone calls to interview French people. So, often when I was covering a tough story, I would dread having to pick up the phone for an interview, especially if it was about something difficult or sensitive. I didn't even know the word for raw bacon, for God's sake - how did I get to be interviewing French people on the phone? And let's not forget, the phone is harder than face-to-face conversations because you miss all the visual cues.

In those early days, by insane luck, a lot of the people I rang spoke English, or at least good enough English to fill in the gaps for me. But often they didn't, and I massacred their language just as I had massacred the fruit flies. Shamefully, regretfully, and with a great deal of embarrassment I butchered the French language, so badly sometimes that the person on the other end just went silent. Yes, my French was atrocious, and I felt guilty about it. This wasn't just going into a bakery and ordering a croissant. Who cares if you get that wrong, especially if you're just a tourist and you're never going to see the baker again. Get your croissant and run, I say. But when you're in a little office where everyone can hear everything you say, speaking French on the phone felt like being naked.

So it was a relief when the new semester of language classes began. And there I was, studying again and realizing that there's nothing more boring than learning French at a school in France - at least if you do it at a traditional school with traditional teaching methods. I'd hunted down a cheap course not far from my office in the 19th arrondissement. Twice a week after work I'd go to the class, but twice a week I'd dread that too. The teacher I had was as fastidious with his verb conjugations as he was with his facial grooming. And he was horrible. I don't think he *meant* to be horrible, he was probably perfectly friendly outside the class, but I think he taught us the same way he'd been taught at school himself - and as I understand it, learning in France is not a process that's meant to be enjoyed. The teacher would throw grammar rules at us and hoped they'd stick. He'd go through example sentences on the board, then whip around the room asking students in turn if they could conjugate the verbs. I never knew the answers, and would plan ahead to try and find the correct response to the teacher's question. When it got to me, I'd often have no idea and would just guess. But if someone got it wrong, he wouldn't explain it. He wouldn't *teach* it. He'd just wait until the student eventually got the right answer.

The irritating part for me was that at this point, I wasn't skilled enough to discuss the topic, the problem, or even why I couldn't answer it. I could only sit silently, like many of the other students. When you're learning a language, one of the biggest achievements is reaching the level where you can explain *what* you don't understand. It's a huge moment. Sure, you might be way off fluency, but a new world opens up when you can say: "Hang on, what does *that* particular word mean? I've never heard *that one* before."

I still hadn't reached that crucial turning point, and my teacher with his overplucked eyebrows wasn't making life easier for me. I remember one time he was going around the room asking students to conjugate verbs into the subjunctive. It's one of the hardest tenses in the French language, irregular and basically impossible to guess. I decided that instead of guessing, I would just tell him that I didn't know.

"*Oliver, c'est quoi le subjonctif ici?*" he said.

"*Je ne sais pas,*" I responded. I don't know.

The rest of the class waited expectantly.

Then, the teacher did the weirdest thing. He mocked me.

"Oh, Oliver, you don't know?" he said in a high-pitched baby voice. "Well maybe you could try and figure it out."

I wasn't expecting that. But there was no way I could figure it out. So I went for a lighter touch and said that I had no idea at all: *J'ai aucune idée*. And as unbelievable as it was to me, he mocked me again in the same child-like voice.

"Oh, Oliver, you have no idea at all, do you?"

I was so shocked. So *embarrassed*. I was lost for words. I sat there gaping like a stunned mullet while the teacher waited. I knew what he was trying to do. Like some kind of French python toying with an

Australian mouse, he was trying to *squeeze* an answer out of me. But he was doing it all wrong. He was actually squeezing the confidence out of me. Finally, in shame, I broke eye contact with him, and he triumphantly moved on to his next victim.

I eventually gave up on the French classes. I stayed long enough to finish the semester (and pass the final tests, thankfully), but I never went back after that. The teaching wasn't for me and I figured there were better ways to learn. Eventually, through sheer time, effort, and language exchanges, I managed to build up my French to an acceptable level. Fluent by some people's standards, sure. But even years after moving to Paris I wouldn't feel comfortable during a fast-paced conversation at a French dinner party. I suppose it didn't matter at the time, because I wasn't being invited to any.

And just for the record, I still can't use the subjunctive tense.

2.6 Making friends

Nine months had passed since I had moved to Paris, and I was finally settling in. The worst of the admin was over, my grasp of the French language was improving, and I had made a solid group of friends, a mix of expats and French people. Most of us were fish out of water, strangers in a strange land, or strangers in a strange city. Even the French guys, all of whom were originally from elsewhere in France.

A lot of my friends were also Australians, which surprised even me. During four years in Sweden, I'd typically walked in the other direction when I heard an Australian accent. I think it was a mix of wanting to fit in with the Swedes and wanting to feel unique. In Sweden there aren't many Australians at all, and meeting another one ruined my illusion that I was doing something special. Imagine if you were exploring a remote village in Mongolia, then found your neighbour from back home at the village pub. It was like that.

But when I moved to Paris it was different. I knew from the outset that I wasn't unique. There's nothing special about an Australian in Paris, so why try to avoid them? Rather, I found myself embracing them and wanting to spend time with them. What's more, they'd been through the same challenges I was facing with opening bank accounts, getting social security, paying taxes. Some of them even had the benefit of a French partner, which made the journey easier for them, and sometimes for me too (indirectly).

In any case, my group of friends in Paris all lived in a big triangle, with the Canal Saint-Martin at the centre. Naturally, the canal proved to be the magnet that would draw us all in, a watering hole where we could grab a beer or a wine. Oftentimes, when the weather was good, we would sit by the canal with a picnic dinner and chat away into the night, like the Parisians did. It wasn't strictly a summer activity either. As the autumn came and went, we continued to congregate at the canal, savouring the last moments of sunshine and preparing for another winter.

In mid-November, in what seemed like the last of the warm weather for the year, I headed back to Sweden for a weekend to tie up loose ends and hang out with Lina. And, as it happened, almost my entire group of friends had decided to take a weekend away as well, all separately. That's the thing with international crowds - they all have a second home to visit, or in-laws to see, or will jump to explore nearby European cities. Even my editor had decided to head back to England for the weekend. We were all taking one last little holiday before the Christmas break at a typically quiet time of the year. And it was during that weekend that Paris as the world knew it was to forever change.

2.7 Terror in Paris

I was in Stockholm on the night Paris was attacked. In fact, I was in a theatre watching a musical. And I had an uncomfortable feeling throughout it. I couldn't put my finger on it, but something felt wrong. It may have just been the all-too-familiar feeling for journalists of going too long without checking their cell phone. When the show finished, I took my phone out of my pocket and saw there were way, way too many notifications. Dozens of missed calls, loads of texts and emails, and the first of the many news flashes from the French news sites.

"Shots fired in Paris."

"Dozens injured in Paris."

"Several killed in Paris attack."

And that was just the beginning.

It was the night that would change Paris and I wasn't there. At the time I learned of the attacks, I had a journalist's response and my first thought was that we had no one to cover what seemed like an enormous story. The editor was in the remote countryside of the UK with no internet. I was in Sweden. That was our entire team at that point. I raced for my laptop and saw the news flashes as they started streaming in. More and more victims. More and more and more. 30, 40, 50. The updates came all night. 60, 70, 80.

For those first hours I was in an almost robotic journalist mode, filtering out the emotions to concentrate on writing the tragic news. I was seeing the horrific footage on social media, scanning frantically through the French press, translating whatever the officials were saying, and telling the news to the enormous number of people around the world who were reading about it.

As the night wore on, and the scale of the attacks became clear, the strangest whirlwind of emotions was going through my mind. The first was the shock. The second was wondering if everyone was OK. My phone, like everyone else's in Paris, was flooded with messages from friends and family around the world. "We just heard what happened, are you alright?" I got the same form of messages from people I hadn't talked to in years. Facebook rolled out a "mark as safe" feature, in which people in Paris could tick a box to show they were alive. It was an unheard of move for Facebook to make, and the company would later face criticism for it, but it certainly seemed at the time the quickest way to let people know if you were safe.

The third strongest emotion for me was disbelief that the series of attacks were not only so indiscriminate, but in the exact areas where I spent my social time in Paris. Four of the bars that were hit were in the canal area where we always hung out. My mind wandered. I'd have been out if I were in Paris on that Friday night. Where would I have been?

But I was so swept up in covering the story that my mind mostly stayed in news mode. 90, 100, 110 dead. My phone was ringing off the hook, news stations from around the world calling for updates. The international journalists couldn't speak French, so they were calling our paper to hear it in English. I stopped answering the phone.

One call I did answer was from my neighbour Stephane. He rang, worried for me, asking where I was, but there was a real trouble in his voice.

"I'm fine, I'm in Stockholm," I said. "But what about you, are you OK?"

"Yes, I'm OK. But I was at the stadium tonight," he said.

Shit. I remembered him talking about going to the soccer match at the Stade de France. It, too, was a target that night.

"It was horrible," he said. "We heard an explosion. No one knew what was happening. No one told us anything. We got back to Paris and ran all the way home. There are police everywhere, everywhere."

A suicide bomber had blown himself up outside the Stade de France stadium, where 80,000 people were watching the game. The bomber managed to kill a security guard and himself. He never made it inside the stadium.

But by far the worst was at the Bataclan, a concert hall in the 11th arrondissement, where gunmen and suicide bombers killed 89 concert goers. I felt sick writing about it and even to this day I still struggle to comprehend it.

I stayed up through the night, reporting on the terror. And that was just the "What" part of the story. The "How", the "Who", and especially the "Why" would take months, even years to cover.

I was on a flight back to Paris the next day. To my home. Which on the one hand felt extremely foreign to me, yet more "home" than it ever had. It was a strange time to be a new resident in Paris. I'd lived there for almost a year, but I had never considered myself Parisian, even though I lived in the centre of the city, had a job there, and had no plans of leaving. But I felt a kind of belonging and a closeness with my friends and with the locals. The Parisians had been strong and resilient in the face of the Charlie Hebdo attacks earlier that year, but would it be the same now that the attack had been so huge and so indiscriminate? 130 people were killed. How *can* you respond to that?

And whether Paris was home to me or not (and how do you define home anyway?), one thing was for sure. When I arrived in Paris to cover the Charlie Hebdo attacks, I had no context of the city. I didn't know what Charlie Hebdo was. I didn't know what anything really meant. But I did know exactly what it meant that a huge number of young people in the 10th and 11th arrondissements were massacred at bars, restaurants, and in a concert hall, all in my neighbourhood. But I was far, far from understanding *why* it happened. And to this day, I still can't.

2.8 Paris after the terror

The months following the terror attacks were unusual. There were so many questions about it all. How could anyone do that to other people? And why would they?

It was a testing time for all Parisians, and a difficult time to be a journalist in Paris. We spent every hour at work covering some aspect of the attack. Who were the victims? What were the ramifications for us all in Paris? What was to happen next? France declared a state of emergency - what did that mean? Who was the terrorist that survived, and how the hell did he get away like that? How did they get their weapons? How was France's Muslim community reacting to the increase in hate crimes against them?

That was our life as reporters. All other news took a break for months. And as much as the city was trying to get back to normal, everyone knew it would take a long time. Some people looked for distractions. Others dwelled on the attacks. Some left the city for good. Tens of thousands of tourists, probably more, were scared away from the City of Light, and Paris suffered from that too. But what I noticed most was that many, many people got on with it. They flocked to the bar terraces for drinks, despite the November cold. Once again, Paris was resilient. The big difference between the response to this attack and the one at Charlie Hebdo was that there was no massive march afterwards: the president had banned public gatherings as part of the state of emergency that was to last two years. Yes, Paris had changed, and soon it would become common to see heavily armed soldiers patrolling the streets. For months, we'd have our bags searched as we went into shopping centres and cinemas. And everyone got used to it. There was no other choice, really.

And gradually, very gradually, life got back to normal.

CHAPTER THREE

———

The French countryside,
difficult bankers, and
a blowout birthday
party in a castle.

3.1 Birthday plans

"You should hire a castle for your 30th birthday," said Shelly, an American friend in Paris. "You can totally get them cheap in the French countryside."

Even though I'd spent over a year in Paris at this point, these kind of sentences still sounded odd to me. I suppose it was something to do with my upbringing in Australia, where we don't have things like old castles in the countryside. We don't have any old buildings at all, really. Not like in Europe. In fact, the oldest thing in my Australian hometown was the lady next door. I wonder whatever happened to her.

"It's simple, you just type *chateau* into AirBnB and set it to France," Shelly continued, snapping me back to the room. "If everyone chipped in, you could get something amazing for a full weekend."

Several months had passed since the attacks and people were looking for distractions. The trauma had brought many people closer together, including my own group of friends. None of us had shown any signs of wanting to leave Paris. Myself, I'd signed to extend the lease on my apartment for another year. But everyone wanted something to look forward to, and a weekend at a chateau seemed like the right kind of idea.

In fact, renting a chateau in the French countryside was exactly the kind of outrageous thing you *should* do when you turn 30 in Paris; I agreed. So I opened the AirBnB app and did as she said. It turned out that there were over 200 properties for rent in France listed as "castles". They were spread all over the country, some tucked among the other luxury homes on the Riviera, others nestled in the hillsides of Brittany, and some only a short drive from Paris. These chateaux ranged from as little as €107 to €8,600 a night. So our challenge was to find one that wouldn't break the bank for anyone - yet would still be grand enough to make for an impressive birthday weekend.

I settled on the Chateau d'Autricourt, which was somewhere in the Champagne region, around 250 kilometres to the east of Paris. We scrolled through the pictures online. Chandeliers, four-poster beds, and enough space for 40 guests. But what really sold it for us was the poetic and enigmatic description on the chateau's website. It spoke of nude nymphs at the nearby stream, a moat filled with enormous carp, an ancient kitchen, ghost hunting, and succulent snail tasting.

"Built on 11th century foundations, but mostly in a Renaissance style, 15 bedrooms, three salons, a vaulted dining room and a medieval kitchen are surrounded by 25 hectares of cow meadows, gamey woods and fish-filled rivers. The decor of your dreams awaits you in this magical atmosphere," it said.

While my birthday wasn't for months to come, I emailed the owners and reserved the chateau. This would be a birthday to remember. And why *shouldn't* we party like it's 1599?

3.2 The basketballers

Playing basketball in Paris opened more doors for me than pretty much anything else. I've played since I was a boy so I'm no slouch on the court. And what's more, while my height made showering at home a nightmare, it was pretty damn helpful on the court. Just being tall meant that I'd often be the first pick for a team, even if no one had seen me play. I shot hoops every weekend when the weather allowed it and I soon became a familiar face on the outdoor court in the Marais. But not everyone warmed to me, and I suspect this was because of a particularly embarrassing language blunder.

But first, a bit of context about the Paris basketball community, which is unlike others I've seen around the world. For starters, many of the French players want to seem tough and cool. They love the American basketball style and often wear the jerseys of current players, the newest sneakers, and play American rap music from portable speakers attached to their phones. When a player arrives at the court, he will walk the length of the magnificent Philippe Auguste wall, and he will "check" every other player, even if they've not met before. By check, I mean he will give them a casual but strong high five, followed by a fist bump - almost like gently punching each other in the fist. And I have no problem at all with that; I think it's pretty cool, actually. Certainly a lot cooler than guys I played with in Sweden, who would give each other a hug before the game like it was some kind of yoga retreat.

The French guys love to use slang with each other too, which fits in pretty nicely with the fist-bumping, tough guy attitude. When I first came across *verlan,* the infamous backwards slang, I almost tripped over my own shoes. I had sunk a long shot and a guy came up to me, bumped my fist, and said what sounded like "bien wedgj" or perhaps "bien wezzhh". I suppose no one knows how to spell it because it's not really a word. At least, it definitely wasn't a word I'd heard before. My teammate, sensing my confusion, told me it was *verlan,* or backwards slang, for *bien joué* ("well played"). So instead of saying *bien joué,* he switched the *joué* around and made it sound more like *wedge.* Get it? (*Joué* sounds like zhoo-way, which becomes ooway-zh - or "wedge.") Confused? Well, so was I! And all I was trying to do was play basketball. All *verlan* words are made by switching the syllables or sounds around in words. An easier example is how the word for thank you, *merci,* becomes *cimer.* People actually say that! And while this might sound like some kind of secret code for children, French people use it a lot, provided they are under the age of 40. Me, I was floundering in the language, but always listening and always learning from these Parisian hoopers.

The guys also had a wide variety of ways to address each other - and never by name. Where in America you might say dude, or where Australians say mate, the French have seemingly endless options. Some of them are *mec,* as I've mentioned before, and which is probably the most common; *gar* (short for *garçon,* or boy); *grand* (as in big); *pote, poto,* and *bro* (which they just took from English). They also love to add the word *mon,* (meaning "my") at the start, similar to how some Americans will call each other "my man", or I suppose how Brits might say "my good man". In any case, you can add the *mon* in front of almost all the slang words above, except one. Which I learned the hard way.

So, while there is no problem with saying *mon grand, mon pote,* or *mon gar* - and they said all of these on repeat - you absolutely cannot say *mon mec,* which actually means "my love" or "my darling", more or less. I had no idea, of course, and trying to fit in I would walk the length of the wall and high-five all the guys while saying the French version of "Hello, my love" to each of them. They maybe looked at me strangely, but that was nothing new. The weirdest thing is that no one ever corrected me. Not until much, much later when I emailed a French friend and began the email with "Salut mon mec". He responded that I should never utter the phrase again unless I either had a boyfriend or wanted to start a fight. At that point, I'd been saying *mon mec* for months. Maybe the guys were all too cool to help a struggling foreigner with his blunders, maybe they didn't care, or maybe they thought I was gay. Who knows?

Anyway, some of my "little darlings" on the court became good friends. I'd heard them talking of an almost mythical indoor league in the Marais and I was itching for an invite. I say mythical because the buildings in central Paris are so narrow that the idea of playing basketball inside one of them seemed impossible. But when my invite finally arrived, basketball became an even more magical experience. The courts were housed inside a stone building called the Halle des Blancs Manteaux, which was over 200 years old and used to be the local covered market. I found an illustration of the building from around 1820 and it's hardly changed. The hall had kept its grand archway entrance and the roof is still supported by enormous stone pillars, which are now separating the two courts. On summer nights we'd be blinded by the sunlight coming in through windows that seemed worthy of a cathedral.

Spots in the league were hard to get, but once you were in you were in for life. The games were every Tuesday night and I played there for years. Often, I'd go out for a drink or two with some of the guys afterwards, particularly two of them who were from Normandy. They who introduced me to Ricard, a drink made from aniseed that's mixed with water and washes down easily after a few hours of basketball. They'd take great pride in this little ritual, using tongs to put the ice in tall tumblers, pouring the Ricard over the top, then adding just the right amount of water so that it wasn't spoiled.

They also led me through the minefields of French slang and other language mishaps. Often, we'd end up in hysterics discussing our worst mistakes, hours into the night. One told me he'd left his English-speaking colleagues in tears after saying pet sleeve, instead of pet peeve. Another told me that he never used the English word *focus* because he couldn't, for the life of him, make it sound like anything besides f&%k us.

"I was giving a presentation in English and trying to get some Americans to pay attention. I said: 'I really need you to focus. Focus hard'. At least I got their attention," he said, as we all roared with laughter.

People have often asked me for tips for integrating into Paris - and especially meeting French people - and I always suggest a group activity like a sport. Even better if it's the kind of activity that can end in drinks afterwards to loosen the tongue and hide the shame of the eternal language learning struggle. Without basketball, I sometimes wonder just how many Parisians I'd actually know.

3.3 Brittany with Fabien

If you want to learn French in Paris, don't hang out with expats. This was a lesson I'd come to learn from Fabien, a sailor from Brittany. Well, he wasn't a sailor, but he *had* been in the navy, and "Fabien the Breton Sailor" had a ring to it. Fabien, with his penchant for hats and his thick beard, was about as French as you could get. But after a decade in London he had decided that he preferred to hang out with English-speaking expats in Paris. One day we were having a canal-side drink and I was talking about my lack of exposure to the French language and the real France.

"Mate, why don't you come out to Brittany? Come and stay with my family for the weekend. That'll give you a real taste of the French language, France, and most importantly, Brittany," he said.

I'd heard about Breton pride. A survey once found that people from Brittany were more likely to consider themselves Bretons first, French second.

"Really? I'd love to come to Brittany," I responded. "I've heard great things about the whole region."

Fabien's eyes filled with pride. There's no quicker way to a Breton's heart than to praise his region. Or his cider. Fabien excitedly pulled out his phone and scrolled through his calendar. This was no empty gesture, this was a plan. By the end of the evening, we'd booked three train tickets from Paris to the French countryside. Lina was coming too.

"You won't regret this, mate, there's nowhere in the world like Brittany," Fabien said.

"Should we order a cider to celebrate?" I responded.

"No, don't drink the cat piss cider in Paris. If it's not Breton cider then it's not worth drinking. You'll soon know the difference."

On the day of the big trip, France was in the middle of a fairly typical summer rail strike. Rail workers weren't happy with something or other, and most of the trains were cancelled, including our train to Rennes, the capital of Brittany. I was covering the strike for the news site during the day and I texted Fabien to let him know about the cancellation.

"Don't worry mate, we'll find a way. Meet at the station as planned, see you at 6."

We all met at Gare Montparnasse, a train station on the Left Bank. A little-known fact outside of France is that all the main train stations in Paris serve specific areas. Trains from Gare du Nord head to the north (nord) of France. Gare de l'Est serves the east (est). And trains from Gare du Lyon go to... you guessed it, Lyon and its surroundings.

Gare Montparnasse (which was called Gare de l'Ouest when it opened) serves Brittany and the west of France - and the whole area around the station has a strong Breton influence. The best *galettes* in town can be found at stands and restaurants dotted around the station. If you want cider, that's where you should head. But I learned all this much later. I was just focusing on getting to the station on time.

When we arrived, the departures board made it crystal clear. Almost all of the trains were cancelled. But a fascinating thing happens when you travel with a Frenchman. You learn how to play the system. Fabien approached the ticket seller, who was clearly exhausted and irritated after spending his day dealing with irate customers. Fabien talked to him politely and calmly.

"We've booked tickets for the 6.30 train to Rennes, which I see is cancelled. Now, there's one other train that's going to Rennes at 7pm..." he began.

"Yes monsieur, but it's fully booked. Not only that, everyone at this station wants to get on that train, because they all want to get to Brittany this weekend."

"I understand," Fabien responded. "But I wanted to know which platform the train will leave from."

The ticket seller looked suspiciously at Fabien and his two tourist friends.

"It's platform four, but it shouldn't serve you any purpose to know it. You don't have a ticket for that train, monsieur, so why would you be getting on it?"

"But of course, merci beaucoup." Fabien smiled, thanked the man, and left.

"OK, let's go to platform four," Fabien told us with a smile. "We're getting on that train."

We headed to the platform in the main hall, where scores of Bretons were spread out widely, all with their eyes on the departure board. Fabien did the same, but from the safety of the entrance to platform four.

"What's going on?" I asked.

"Everyone in this crowd wants to get on that train, but there's not enough room for us all," he said. "It's first come, first served. As soon as that sign reveals which platform the train leaves from, it'll be a blind panic as everyone rushes to the platform. But we know which platform it is, the man told us."

Even though we were apparently at the right platform, Fabien kept his eyes on the departure board, just like everyone else. Me, I observed the crowd. Would-be travellers. Tired Bretons. All desperate to get on that one train for Brittany. And suddenly, a ripple of panic hit the crowd. The departure board had clicked over and prompted a stampede. Bretons were scrambling over each other, elbowing their way forward, and barging towards the platform. And they were all running towards us. I looked up at the board. Rennes, Brittany: Platform Four. Fabien smiled. We were at the front of the crowd, and we got on the train as soon as the doors opened. Sure, we didn't have tickets, but neither did most of the others. We headed for the bar, as all the actual seats were taken by those lucky enough to have booked the 7 pm train. The rest of us who managed to get on board filled up the bar and the spaces between the carriages. The Bretons remaining on the platform weren't so lucky and were eventually refused permission to board.

"These rail strikes are an embarrassment," Fabien admitted as the train pulled away from the station. "But there's one piece of good news.

Because our train was cancelled, I'll be claiming a refund for us all. This is a free trip to Brittany! And what's more, we're already in the bar."

If I'd have been travelling alone, I probably wouldn't have even tried to get on the train. I'd have been on a bus, or staying home for the weekend. Who'd have thought travelling with a Frenchman could open such doors? And I soon learned that there's no better way to see Brittany than with a Breton.

Fabien's family lived in a village near Saint-Brieuc, the small town where he grew up. The town isn't famous for anything unless you are a big fan of the annual Tour de France cycling race, which sometimes passes through. But from the moment we stepped into Fabien's house, I was hit by the feeling of actually being in France for the first time. Sure, walking down the cobbled streets of Montmartre, or sitting on a cafe terrace in the Left Bank of Paris both felt very French. But Paris isn't France, and France isn't Paris - as anyone from either side would be quick to tell you.

Fabien's mother welcomed us as their pet dogs jumped at our legs. And his mother, as a rule, decided she wouldn't speak a word of English with us, even though she probably could have done.

"There's no better way to learn French than to immerse yourself," she said.

Fabien's family served us hot galette pancakes with cheese and sausage, typical Breton food. We drank locally made cider, and we talked long into the night about the differences between France, Australia, and Sweden.

As the night drew to an end, part of me was sad to realize that I couldn't understand France the way I could if I had French in-laws like so many other expats did. I didn't have a family out in the French countryside who'd point out the idiosyncrasies of the French, the tricks to the best recipes, or the meaning of certain gesticulations. The thing is - it's exceptionally difficult to figure out a country when you don't have close access to one of its families. French friends are great, and they can teach you a lot, but it's not the same thing. As I observed the Brittany skies from Fabien's childhood bedroom, I was beginning to realize that I might never understand France and the French without such an opportunity.

Luckily, way down the line, I would start a podcast all about figuring out France, a podcast that would teach me and hundreds of thousands of listeners about this fascinating country. But at this point I was still just a humble journalist struggling to find my way. My mind drifted as I breathed fresh country air and as the stars came out in the Brittany sky.

3.4 The countryside

We woke up the next morning to a full French breakfast. The table was laid out with fresh bread, homemade jam, and plenty of pastries.

"Eat up, eat up," said Fabien's mother. "There's plenty left and we've got a lot to do today."

We spent the day exploring the coastal towns of Brittany, including the magnificent fortified Saint Malo. On the way home, we came to an unusually named town, Erquy. It was a small and quiet place, perched by the seaside and dotted with cafes, bars, and restaurants.

"This town should be famous," Fabien said, shaking his head, as we sat down for another cider. "Have you heard of Asterix, the comic? Well take a look around. You're in the comic book! This is the town that is said to have inspired it all. But you'd never know."

He was right. After the cider we took a look around, but there wasn't even a vague hint that it was connected to one of the world's most famous comic books. Not even a gift shop with little Asterix toys. Or postcards. I couldn't believe it. Not least because the French are obsessed with comic books, or *bandes dessinées* as they're known here. But Erquy didn't seem to care. In some countries they'd rename such a place "Asterix Town" and watch the tourists fly in. There'd be Obelix ice-cream and magic potion cocktails. But in Erquy there was nothing.

"The funniest thing," Fabien said, "is that someone once made an enormous stone statue of Obelix - you know, the big one who fell in the magic potion as a baby - and they offered it to the town as a gift. But the town refused it. They didn't want it. And I've got no idea why."

He gazed out to sea, perhaps reflecting on his days in the navy. Simpler times. Without the mainland hassles of Paris. The fickle Erquy residents. The rail strikes.

"So what happened to the giant statue?" I asked.

"Oh my step-dad took it. It's sitting in the back garden of his bed-and-breakfast in a nearby town. It makes no sense that it's there, but my step-dad quite likes it."

And so it was, as we saw later in the afternoon. A mammoth stone statue of Obelix, the kind of thing that could have stood proudly in a park in the middle of Erquy. But it was in the middle of a garden in the middle of nowhere, without even an explanation.

The weekend was drawing to a close, so we headed back to Fabien's village to get a good night's sleep before taking the early train to Paris.

Of course, that train was cancelled too - the strikes were apparently still on - so we hopped on board another, and rode in the bar carriage once again. As the Brittany countryside rushed by the bar window, I got to thinking about the region, the local pride, and the Obelix statue. The French are a proud bunch, and none are prouder than those outside of Paris. But while they'll bleed in the colours of their flag, they're not going to force anything on you. Maybe they don't want our tourist dollars. Maybe they don't all want statues of Obelix and postcards of Asterix. It seemed to me that people in the countryside were quite happy to leave the tourists to Paris and Disney World. Sure, my first trip to "the real France" was only a weekend, but I felt like I was coming back to Paris with a deeper understanding of the country.

No, France isn't Paris and Paris isn't France. And everyone in the country seems pretty happy to keep it like that.

3.5 French kissing

As I pulled into Lyon on a warm summer afternoon Chantelle waved to me from the window of her second-floor apartment. She buzzed me into her building, I climbed the stairs, and she flung open the door to greet me. And then we kissed. Right on the lips.

Now, while this might sound like a romantic start to chapter 3.5, I'm afraid you're getting it all wrong, just like I was. You see, I'd never met Chantelle before. I'd never even seen her. Chantelle was nothing more than the owner of the apartment that I was renting for the weekend. So why were we kissing on the lips? Well, I wondered the same thing, and Lina, who was standing beside me, wasn't looking too impressed.

"Oh la la, I'm so sorry," Chantelle said, blushing. "But I see what has happened. It's *la bise*, it's different here. In Lyon, we start the greeting kisses on the right hand side. You should move your own head right, then left. Not left then right, like in Paris."

So what had happened was that as I moved my head to the left to kiss the air by Chantelle's right cheek (as they do in Paris), she had moved her head to to her right to kiss my left cheek. And as a result, our air kiss greeting turned into a good old fashioned mouth-to-mouth smooch.

This was all a bit unfair, if you ask me. I had spent a long time in Paris accepting and eventually getting comfortable with the air-kissing custom. But I'd never considered it could be a whole different dance across France. And while my first visit to Lyon was lovely, it was the cheek kissing that stayed with me. The very concept that such a fundamental French custom could be reversed in different towns fascinated me. In fact, the whole matter of cheek-kissing seemed to get more complicated the closer I looked into it. And let me just say, if you think it all sounds pretty simple, then you either don't understand it, or you're a genius. Here's my take on how it works.

The basic idea is that when you meet someone of the opposite sex in France, you touch cheeks with them and make a kissing noise in the air. Then repeat this for the other cheek. Easy enough, right?

Wrong. Here are the exceptions to the rule.

If they're from outside of Paris, they may kiss more, or fewer, times.

Non-Parisians *may* start on the right instead of the left.

Tourists and expats might be uncomfortable with kissing.

Now, if he's a man and you're a man, you need to *earn* the kiss. There are a few ways you can attain kissing status with another Frenchman.

4a) You are a close relative to the Frenchman. Brother, father, son, or cousin.

4b) You get to know them closely or have married into their family.

I'm rather captivated by the topic. And if you think I'm exaggerating the complexity of *la bise*, well let me tell you that if anything I'm underplaying it. Just take a look at point one above and think about it. If you're from Paris, you kiss twice, left then right. If you're from the south of France then you kiss three times. Now, what happens when a Parisian and a Provençal meet on holiday in the west of France, where you're allegedly supposed to kiss four times? Is there an air kiss where someone goes in for the third when the other is retreating to start some small talk? Or do they just *know*, because that's how it is?

Point two is intriguing too, the whole "Which side to start on?" thing. I'll never forget my awkward smooch with Chantelle, but I also wonder how many times that happens among French people.

Point three above, the whole expat thing, that can ruin a lot, too. You're at a party with a mix of French people and expats, and you go around the room kissing the girls and shaking hands with the boys. You're meeting them for the first time, so you have no idea where they're from. You come to a Swedish woman. There's every chance that as you lean in for the kiss she will offer you her hand to shake (gender equality above all else!). She might even go for the more traditional Swedish hug as a force of habit. And if everyone doesn't play along with the kissing game, someone is bound to look stupid.

I have a friend, Cyril, who is from Nice on the Mediterranean coast. We are on kissing terms now (although of course we weren't at first). But in Nice, they start on the right. So every time I go in to kiss him, we end up meeting in the middle, just like with the woman in Lyon. I bring it up nearly every time. "You're not in Nice anymore, Cyril, adapt," I say. But he doesn't care. He had the last laugh once when he invited me to a party in Paris with all his family and friends from Nice. Every single one of them went to the right for the first kiss when I met them. So I gave up and went right for the night too.

But of all the twists and turns of this little dance, the part I find the most interesting is the idea of earning the kiss from another Frenchman. A friend of mine from Toulouse, Arnaud, explained it to me.

"If, say, we were to get really drunk tonight and end up swimming in the canal, we'd kiss from that point on. If we went out on a wild bender of a night, we'd kiss afterwards too," he told me.

"So it's about alcohol, then?"

"No, it's more about going through some kind of adventure or ordeal together. When you both come out on the other side, you just know that it's time to start kissing. It's almost like you've become a brother," he said.

What a minefield! My mind was racing, as usual, with the idea of earning the kiss from French friends. Of ducking, diving, swimming in canals, going on adventures, having a true French brother at the end of it all.

Unfortunately, it never happened with Arnaud. In fact, I rarely see him anymore. Since we chatted about kissing that day by the canal, three years ago, Arnaud has gotten married and has two kids. When I occasionally see him, we simply shake hands. I can't help wondering what adventures we missed.

3.6 The bank

My September birthday was fast approaching and I'd booked the chateau for it. Life was too short not to, I figured. I got a guest list together and told everyone that for €120 each, we could spend the weekend living like kings and queens (with food and alcohol included). A few dozen people confirmed they were in. Money was still tight for me, as usual, but I had enough to cover the cost of renting the chateau, provided of course, that everyone paid me back straight away. Perhaps I didn't stress the urgency of the situation enough, because almost no one transferred their share upfront. I found this out when I got a call from the bank to tell me my balance was dangerously low. So low, in fact, that I had negative money in the bank. I was well beyond a month's rent in the negatives, and the bank wanted to talk about it.

Now I don't know how it works in the country you're in, but where I'm from, when you run out of money your bank card stops working. Quite simple, really. But nothing is simple in France. In fact, I'd never even considered a negative bank balance to be a possibility. And how did it get so far into the negatives, I wondered. I mean, I obviously rented a chateau, but I thought I had enough to cover the deposit. I went into the bank to enquire why I owed them so much money. The woman at the desk explained.

"Well, monsieur, you've gone into the negatives on your balance, and you're not allowed to do that," she said.

"But why is it so far negative?" I asked. I surely hadn't frittered away *that much* while I was watching my spending.

"Well, every time you've used your card since you went under zero, we've simply charged you 20 euros as a fee."

A €20 fee? The banker printed out my statement and proved to me that this was exactly what she had done. We perused it together.

"See, here you bought something for €1 at a supermarket. We charged you €20 for that. That same day you bought something for €1.30. We charged you another €20."

"But... but... I was just buying milk. Why didn't you tell me that I was in the negatives?" I asked. "If I'd known that you would charge me, I wouldn't have used the card to buy milk."

Let's stop here for a second and be brutally honest. That sentence above is a tremendously tricky one to say if you're still learning French. It's what my French teacher would have called the future conditional tense - "If I had known, I wouldn't have…". But I had never learned it properly, so obviously I didn't say it correctly. My mind flashed back to my mocking French teacher and I shuddered.

In any case, verb tenses and teachers aside, I wasn't getting anywhere. The Frenchwoman didn't care that I was being charged €21.30 for a bottle of milk. She even seemed a tiny bit pleased about it. And it was at this precise moment that I learned the importance of having a strong argument if you want to get your way in France. And unfortunately, I learned this because I absolutely didn't have a strong argument. I had nothing. Just bewilderment. And a growing feeling of despair. I considered getting angry, just like my downstairs neighbour had done with the internet people, but I decided my French still wasn't up to scratch.

The banker gave me the "that's how it is" shrug that I was coming to know so well. I considered pleading my case a little, but I figured I'd think it over instead. So I left. That night, I was having a canal-side beer with a Parisian *mec* called Clovis (no kiss, firm handshake, two pumps). Clovis shared his name with the first King of the Francs and had the charm of a TV host. Well, he was a TV host actually. He was also born in Paris - a rare breed in the French capital, where so many locals are actually born elsewhere in the country. I told Clovis my plight and he wasn't impressed.

"No one should have to put up with that kind of nonsense. Let me pay a visit to your bank manager. I'll sort this out. Just tell me when and where."

The next day, I saw a performance unlike any I've seen before or since. Clovis, dressed up in a suit and tie, strode into the bank and took no prisoners. He played the good cop *and* the bad cop. He switched from "Hello, mademoiselle, how are you today?" to "You know as well as I do that my client can leave your tiny bank for a dozen others that wouldn't be hassling him with this kind of rubbish." It was incredible to watch. The banker couldn't keep up with him. Every time she got defensive or upset, he turned the charm back on and she melted like a cheese fondue. Like a chess grandmaster, he was knocking down her pieces one by one. *Bam*, there goes another pawn. She backpedalled, and then *boom*, she lost her bishop, then her knight. It was quite the sight. Eventually, he convinced her that the bank had been unreasonable and that something would have to be done about it or we'd walk. And it worked. By the time we left, the banker had erased all the fees and made it so my account could sink as far as minus €2,500 before I'd incur further charges. Checkmate! I was dumbfounded. The first time around it was the banker who had won. But this time we beat the bank. Thanks to Clovis, named after the King of the Francs; now more like the King of the Banks.

"Thanks for doing that for me, it was a treat to watch," I said. "It's amazing that that's what it takes to get things done in this country."

Clovis just smiled and gave me a Gallic shrug of his own.

"That's how it works in France. Now where are we going for lunch? On you, I think."

3.7 The chateau

Everyone should rent a chateau in the French countryside before they die. When we did it for my thirtieth birthday, it was every bit as magical, mythical, and mad as it may sound. The guests still talk about it to this day. The expectations were high as we all took Friday off work, rented cars, and headed out into the countryside. Our castle - the Chateau d'Autricourt - was in Burgundy, a few hours southeast of Paris. I was in a minivan with four other people, plus supplies for the whole crowd. The van was so full that we drove with food between our legs and wine bottles tucked between the seats. The excitement was almost tangible. As we zipped through the fields of the Champagne region, we got to talking about the chateau itself and its elegant, mysteriously translated website. Lina pulled up the page and read it aloud.

"Have you ever dreamt of being a princess or a *chatelaine...*" she began.

"What's a *chatelaine*?" I asked Fabien, my walking French/English dictionary.

"Eurgh, well it's someone, a woman actually, who runs a castle," said Fabien.

I made a mental note of yet another wonderful untranslatable French word. Fabien, in the back seat, looked like he was imagining life with a *chatelaine* of his own. Lina continued to read as we passed more vineyards.

"Have you ever dreamt of being a princess or a *chatelaine*, a king or a knight, to let your long blond hair down a tower, or to fight an enemy on a drawbridge and to go treasure hunting afterwards?

"All kinds of dreams are waiting to be manifested in this enchanting place. Bursting with enormous potential, it needs your fantasy and your creativity to be rescued from time's clutches.

"Feast in the medieval 'salle à manger', frolic with picnics in the meadows, take tea in the Indian temple, fish in the moat, savor succulent snail-tasting, breakfast on an open-tower, ghost-hunting... here, everything is possible!"

Everyone went quiet in the car, imagining life in the chateau. Lina was scrolling through the pictures with widening eyes.

When we finally arrived we felt as if we'd hit the castle jackpot. The roads had been getting progressively smaller as ventured further from Paris, and by the time we reached the castle grounds we were well and truly in the middle of nowhere. We drove through the entrance, where huge lime trees flanked the driveway. We passed the ruins of a tower in the fields and continued as the trees thinned and eventually revealed the chateau in all its splendid glory. The exterior was jaw-dropping. We drove across a stone drawbridge over the moat that surrounded the chateau, parked in the courtyard, then tried to take it all in.

On one side was a grand Renaissance building with vine-covered limestone walls and grey slated roofs. The pointed turrets of five towers cast shadows over the inner courtyard. To the other side were more sleeping quarters in a separate building with its own towers and turrets. Between the two was a little chapel, in case anyone decided to get married, I suppose. We could see huge fish swimming lazily in the moat, while the sun shone strong on the hectares of fields in the distance.

With smiles that matched our own, the owners and their dog greeted us for the grand tour. And if we thought the exterior was grand, we were in for a surprise. The *chatelaine*, or the lady who owned the castle, led us into a huge stone kitchen with vaulted walls and a massive raised fireplace.

"Big enough to roast a wild boar," she said with a wink.

The kitchen led into a mammoth dining room with several stuffed ostrich heads attached to the wall by the base of their long necks. On both sides of the room were fireplaces with Gothic chimneys. Beyond the dining room was the grand salon - or the dance floor, I thought - then a games room and a few spare bedrooms. At both ends of the ground floor were staircases leading to long corridors upstairs, which were lined with stuffed wild boar and deer heads. Along the corridors were the doors to the rest of the bedrooms, most of which came complete with four poster beds, aristocratic portraits, open fireplaces, and period bathrooms. It was unreal. Many if not most of the guests got lost at some point over the weekend, which is hardly a surprise considering we lived in such tiny Parisian apartments. Lina and I took the royal suite - it was my birthday party after all - and our ensuite bathroom was bigger than our entire home in Paris. The bedroom was big enough to swing a tiger. We even had our own balcony looking over the fields and the moat with its fat and lazy carp swimming below. And the castle walls were about a metre thick, perfect for keeping the cold out and for containing the noise from any outrageous parties hosted inside.

The guests arrived throughout the day from their various corners of Europe (and Australia) and we arranged everyone into groups of five. Each group was to organize one meal and to clean up after it, and nothing else. The idea was that the serial helpers could take a break and the serial slackers wouldn't be able to get away with any nonsense.

And it seemed to work. We'd bought fairly simple ingredients for feasts, fried chicken, big salads, pastas and it was all washed down with local wine and champagne. Those on breakfast duty were responsible for waking up first, then driving to the village boulangerie to collect our daily order of 15 baguettes, 15 croissants, and 15 pain au chocolats.

In the days we played ball games in the garden, lazed on chaise longues, and bathed in a nearby pond. In the evenings we ate like royalty by a long table in the front garden; my friends gave a mix of warm and cruel speeches to mark my birthday, and we watched the sunset over the French countryside.

And at night we partied like French aristocrats.

Now, I'm not one to condone excesses of any kind, but when I say we partied like aristocrats I'm not exaggerating. The parties were so wild and unruly that most guests don't remember what happened. Fortunately, or perhaps unfortunately, an Australian guest with an interest in amateur photography had positioned a GoPro camera high in a corner of the main dining hall and set it to take a picture every five minutes. It captured details of the night that no one would have otherwise believed. Flicking through them the next day almost left more questions than answers. After dinner, there's a shot of the dining-room turned dancefloor gradually filling up. In the next shot, there's a group of people lingering suspiciously over the champagne, which I assume is the moment someone spiked the proverbial punch with I don't even dare guess what. A few more photos later and another of the Australian guests has captured everyone's attention as she strides into the room in a corset and an enormous, white Marie Antoinette wig. Then the corset is gone and she stands bare-breasted to the shock and delight of the crowd (while her wig remains perfectly in place). In the next, a cake with sparklers has appeared as more people seem to have removed their clothes. As the pictures continued the night apparently turned into some kind of wild rave that ended - as far as I can tell - when a half-naked Marie Antoinette herself can be seen approaching the camera on the wall with her hand outstretched. The GoPro was found tucked between the sofa cushions the next morning, forever taking photos of nothing but pillows. Perhaps it was better that way.

3.8 Nice holiday

It was around this time that things got serious between me and Lina. She had moved out of her place in Belleville and into my tiny apartment. I'd met her parents several times and had even stayed with them in Sweden. What better way to enjoy the last of the good weather for the year than to all take a holiday together in Nice, on the French Riviera?

Nice was as lovely as ever with its stony beach front, wide promenade, and summery sea views. The pace of life, too, was refreshingly slower than in Paris. But best of all, someone had the brainwave to rent scooters for the weekend. Now when I say scooter, I mean the one with an engine, the kind that lets you whizz along the coastline of the Mediterranean sea without a care in the world. That's exactly what we did, and it was one of the most exhilarating experiences of my life. A real game changer. I'd never ridden a scooter before, never even considered trying one. But there was such a wonderful, freeing feeling of zipping along the roads with the air in my face, the wind on my body, and the road stretched out in front of me. I loved driving through the city, weaving among the cars, parking wherever I wanted and then getting back on and doing it all again.

We scooted all over the Riviera that weekend, from Monaco to Antibes and I was a man possessed. Then one warm evening I had a life-changing experience.

We were all driving back to Nice from Antibes after the sun had set and a wild thunderstorm took us by surprise. The thunder bellowed, the lightning was frightening, but the rain was nowhere to be seen yet. We had the Mediterranean sea to our right, an empty coastal road ahead of us, and I never felt more alive. We raced towards the safety of the hotel, trying to beat the inevitable downpour. The roar of the thunder grew stronger. The sky grew darker. It felt like the universe was speaking to me. Shouting at me! I could feel the energy in the air and my body was tingling with vibrations from the scooter, the thunder, and the sheer thrill of being in the middle of a storm. I felt like one of those tornado chasers. We were facing danger, the risk of getting caught in the downpour, or getting struck by lightning, and we were dashing to escape it. All on the back of a scooter, exposed to the elements, and at their mercy. I was yelling with joy, it was ecstasy at 45 kilometres an hour. I felt like a bolt of lightning could have hit me and I wouldn't have even noticed.

We made it back to our hotel before the rain started and I was a changed man. I had a revelation, and I knew exactly what was missing from my life. Right then and there I told Lina and her family that I wanted a scooter of my own for Paris. It would be perfect, I said. But they all looked at me like I was crazy. Lina put her foot down, and quickly.

"Are you mad?" she said. "Do you know how dangerous that would be?"

Her parents joined in. They said that scooting along the empty roads in the Riviera was one thing, but they wouldn't want their daughter to be doing the same in Paris. It was a resounding no and I was surprised, shocked, disappointed, and maybe even hurt. But they talked me out of it and I gradually accepted it.

When we got back to Paris, even though I had given up on the idea of getting a scooter, the topic had created a divide between Lina and me. If I even mentioned it, she changed the subject. And what was worse, the divide spread to other parts of our life. She started to act secretively, snatching up her phone when it got a message, leaving the room to answer calls, slipping out of our Paris apartment with only vague details about where she was going. Yes, the relationship was still in its early stages but something didn't feel right. We'd come to our first big disagreement - but I'd soon learn that there was a wild and surprising explanation for her behaviour.

CHAPTER FOUR

New wheels, leaving
Montorgueil, and
exploring Paris by road.

4.1 The red beast

I was in the office on the day of my 30th birthday when I got an unusual text from Lina.

"Meet me on rue de Rambouillet at 6 pm. Come from Avenue Daumesnil. I'll be waiting for you."

It was an odd message, that much was for sure. I looked up the address; it was in the 12th arrondissement of Paris, where neither of us had any business. I couldn't figure out why she'd invited me there. Curiosity got the better of me and I searched the area online for a clue - but I found nothing. Six o'clock was too early for a dinner date and far too late for a lunch. Could it be an activity? The area was directly beneath the Coulée Verte elevated walkway, but we'd been there and done that. It was also close to the Gare du Lyon train station - perhaps we were going for a train ride? Secretly, I hoped we weren't leaving Paris as I'd organized a small birthday bash at the canal. Yes, we'd already partied in the chateau, but I wanted one last celebration, where the rest of my Paris friends who had missed the castle weekend could come too. But the one thing that bamboozled me the most about Lina's text was: why did I have to approach from one side in particular? What difference would that make?

I finished work and grabbed a bike from the Velib stands and headed south to the 12th arrondissement. Getting to the street itself was a complicated trip, not to mention finding a way to approach it from the south. I had to take a wide turn all the way around the destination, find a place to park the bike, then walk - as I was told - from Avenue Daumesnil. The whole time I was trying to figure out what was going on.

When I approached the meeting point, Lina was standing on the corner of the road with a wicked smile on her face. I glanced around but there was nothing there. Definitely no restaurant or shop, just a kind of small alleyway leading to what looked like a residential area.

"Don't take another step and close your eyes," she said, as if I needed further confusion.

With that, she took my hand, led me around the corner and told me to open my eyes. When I did, I was speechless. Gobsmacked. Dumbfounded! There in front of me, parked to the side of the cobblestone alley, was a red scooter. It was beautiful, shining like a new toy. It had a green and white racing stripe along the side, radiant silver finishes on the front and back, and jet black wheels. Never ridden before. And it was mine. But I didn't understand this at the time. "What? Are we…? What's the…" I was honestly speechless.

"It's yours. It's my gift to you. As long as you don't mind taking me around too, sometimes," she said, pointing to two helmets perched on the scooter seat. One was black, one was speckled gold.

"Mine's the gold one, don't worry," she said, adding that she'd bought them from a Harley Davidson store near Bastille.

At this point I still thought it was some kind of gimmick. That she'd rented the scooter for the afternoon. Surely, surely she hadn't just bought me a scooter for my 30th birthday. She was about as penniless as I was. And if she *did* buy it, then how the hell did she manage? She hardly even spoke French. How did she sort out the registration and insurance…

"I sorted out the registration and insurance, it's all done," she said, reading my mind again. Or maybe I was thinking out loud. "It was a struggle, I can tell you that for free."

I was still speechless. While this all might sound perfectly normal to all you readers who've received new red scooters for their birthdays in Paris, it was a huge moment for me. Not only did I have zero inkling that I was about to become a scooter owner, but I'd never owned anything new like that before. I'd never had a new bicycle, never owned any kind of car, and certainly nothing like a scooter. My mind was zooming as I was trying to process what was happening. The first thing that came into my mind was:

"So, how does it work?"

"I don't know, I haven't driven it," she responded.

"Then how did you get it to this alleyway? And why *are* we in this alleyway, anyway?"

She laughed.

"Well if I told you to meet me at the scooter shop then you'd have figured out the surprise. I just asked the guys to drive it down here, far enough from the shop so you'd never guess what was happening. After all, I've come to know them pretty well. You wouldn't imagine how much work goes into buying a scooter for someone else in Paris."

I sat on the seat, put the key in the ignition, and started her up.

"So, what, do we just drive it away?" I asked, still somewhat unsure of what was happening.

"Well, I think you should figure out how it works first. Take it up and down the alley. Then let's get going, we've gotta christen this thing before we get to your party," she responded, pulling a mini-bottle of champagne from her handbag. What a woman.

After a few spins up and down the alley, Lina jumped on the back and we headed to the Seine River to toast to a new chapter in Paris. We parked the bike by a ramp that led to the water's edge, popped the champagne, then headed on foot to the banks. And it was only about three minutes before I got my first lesson in scooter ownership. Two burly policemen pulled up at the river bank and, even though there were scores of picnicking Parisians, made a beeline towards us.

What's going on? Why us? Was the scooter stolen? Is that how she could afford it?

"*C'est votre scooter, monsieur?*" one of them said to me, gesturing with his head towards the conspicuously red vehicle.

How did he know it was mine? What have I done wrong? Is Lina an outlaw?

"*Oui*," I responded. "It's a birthday present, *she* gave it to me," I said, pointing to Lina and switching to English in the hopes it would throw the police off the scent.

"*Vraiment*? Really? She bought you *that* scooter for your birthday? How old are you?" he asked.

"I'm 30 today," I answered, beaming like a proud child.

Where was this going?

"Well, let me tell you, that's an incredible gift. You're a lucky man. And that's a lovely scooter. But you can't park it there near the emergency exit. You'll have to move it."

We apologized to the officer and we turned to head back to the scooter. The rest of the champagne could wait. But I had another thought.

"Officer, one last question. How did you know that it was *my* scooter? There are hundreds of people here," I said.

"Ah yes, but you are the only ones holding helmets," he responded. "Now, happy birthday and hold onto that woman."

This might sound like an exaggeration, but this is exactly how our scooter life started. The officer was charming, he spoke excellent English, and he was right to tell me to hold on to that woman. But he got one thing wrong. After they left and I started the scooter up for the second time, it was that woman who was holding on to *me* as we zoomed along the Seine River, across the Pont de Sully bridge, and along the length of the Canal Saint-Martin to where my friends were waiting for us. And what better entry to your own Paris birthday party than on your brand new red scooter? I tooted the horn as we pulled up to the cheers of my friends who gathered around and took pictures. As I parked it safely around the corner, Lina and I smiled at one another.

"I'm sorry I was such a louse in Nice, telling you that you shouldn't get a scooter," she said. "It's just that I'd already started the process of buying this one and I had to get you off the scent."

What a woman, I thought again.

I locked the bike, took Lina in my arms, and kissed her on the lips. A proper kiss though, not the accidental Lyon version.

"What a wonderful present, I can't believe you did all that," I said, as we turned and headed back to our friends.

One thing had just been made very clear, very quickly. That vehicle was about to add a whole new dimension to our life in Paris. And far beyond. Indeed, it would be this little scooter, the Red Beast, that would take us 4,000 kilometres around the entirety of France for our honeymoon. We didn't know this at the time, of course. Why, we weren't even engaged yet. But the arrival of the red scooter was about to change our lives, and there was an unmistakable tingle of excitement in the Paris air.

4.2 A car red

While the red scooter quickly became a major character in my Paris life, it was actually a red car that got me interested in learning French. I was 11 years old, living in a small town on the east coast of Australia, and my older brother Tom was telling me about his first lesson in French.

He explained to me that in France they don't say "a red car", they say "a car red". In other words, they put the adjective after the noun, rather than the other way around, as we do in English. I suppose I'd heard French words and maybe even learned a few of them before this conversation with my brother. But the concept that grammar could be so fundamentally different in other languages exploded my 11-year-old mind. I was fascinated.

Now, I had long been a fan of the English language. A huge fan, even. I can clearly remember surprising my teacher when I was about six years old during a lesson on apostrophes. The teacher wrote "it's" on the chalkboard then explained it was short for "it is" and then moved on. But what? She didn't add the obvious, that it was also short for "it has", as in, "it's been a long time". I made sure to tell her, and she looked at me strangely as if to say "What kind of 6-year-old cares about this stuff?" Then she frowned and added "it has" to the board. She probably thought I was an annoying little ragamuffin, but that was just how my mind worked.

Anyway, the point is that still to this day, I am a word nerd. Language is probably my favourite topic. I love that there is a word for the little dot on top of the letter i (it's called a tittle). I wonder if the dot on the letter j is also called a tittle. Writing this now, I wonder if the word tittle could be a verb too, so just as you can say "Don't forget to dot your is and cross your ts", can you say "Be sure to tittle your i's"? The sad shame is that most people don't care about the oddities of language more than about a minute's worth at a time. In fact, I'm probably dangerously close to losing you right now…

In any case, back when I was working at the news site in Sweden, I developed a reputation for writing columns about the Swedish language. And I was happy to write similar stories about French when I joined the team in Paris. For example, I wrote a whole article about the superbly versatile swear word *putain*. Another about the importance of the word *bonjour*. I wrote about curious phrases, expressions, idioms, and sounds. And I was delighted to learn that some French people, especially women, would take a sharp inward breath when saying yes, almost exactly like they did in northern Sweden.

But my favourite language curiosity of all time is the untranslatable word. And before we go any further, let me explain *my* definition of "untranslatable" so we're all on the same page.

An untranslatable word is a foreign word that doesn't have a single-word equivalent in English.

Chatelaine is a good example, where the best and shortest translation is "a woman who runs a castle". How can you fit that into one English word? Impossible! There are loads of great words in French that I consider to be untranslatable. For example, in France people tend to take their summer holidays in July or August. Lengthy, month-long holidays. If you take them in July, or as the French call it, *juillet*, then you're a *juilletiste* (while those who holiday in August are *aoûtiens*). Now, imagine that you can say that singular word - *juilletiste* - to a French person and they'd understand. In English, you'd have to say "a person who holidays in July" - but even then, you're not capturing it. It's more "A person who holidays in July rather than August". And if you think about it, even that doesn't explain it for someone in the southern hemisphere, where July and August are winter months. In France, you can call someone a *juilletiste*. In Australia, you'd have to say "she takes July off for her summer holiday rather than August".

I suppose why I love these little quirks is because they also teach you about the culture that comes with the language. The example above shows that the French take long holidays in the summer, and that the idea is so popular that they have names for which part of the season you holiday in. When you boil it down, you realize that the French take their summer holidays seriously.

Anyway, collecting untranslatable words is one of my favourite things to do. And they're not always charming little insights into a country's vacationing habits. The French have a single word for "cutting someone's throat" (égorger) and also for "throwing someone out a window" (défenestrer).

Another favourite I have, which is pretty difficult to explain if you don't know French, is the verb *tutoyer*, which more or less means "to be less formal with someone". To understand this, though, you have to know that in France there are two ways to say "you". There's the formal version, *vous*, that you'd use with older people or strangers. Then there's the less formal version, *tu*, which you'd use with friends, children, animals. So the verb *tutoyer* more specifically means "to use the tu form". I love this word, *tutoyer*: it's absolutely untranslatable; it says a lot about French culture; and it makes no sense at all to English speakers. And the word *vouvoyer*, which means "to use the vous form", is an equally great and untranslatable word. But maybe we should leave it there, before it gets too confusing.

All this is to say that the French language is a rich thing, and for me it was never more beautiful than the day a senior architect told me I could *tutoyer* her, almost two years after I'd started working in the building. I didn't have to say *vous* any longer, I could finally say *tu*.

There was a rush of emotions, a feeling of pure acceptance, equality, friendship even. I wonder if there's a word to describe the pleasure that comes with social formalities being swept away. But who cares if there's not, it was a lovely feeling to be considered as an equal with one of the older architects, I felt warm and welcome - perhaps for the first time in that office. To this day I'm not sure, but I think the architect chose to accept me because she also rode a scooter around Paris and felt, deep down, that we weren't so different after all.

4.3 A whole new Paris

They say Paris is a city best discovered on foot - but they, whoever they are, have obviously never discovered Paris on scooter. It was amazing how much having that vehicle changed our lives in Paris. Overnight, the city became more manageable. Montmartre was a fifteen-minute ride away. I could get to work in ten minutes. The thought of crossing the river to explore the Left Bank didn't seem like a day trip anymore. We could head to the city's big parks - the Bois de Vincennes and the Bois de Boulogne - without spending half the day on travelling. We made excursions to places we'd never considered visiting before, like the Parc des Sceaux with its explosions of cherry blossoms, and the affluent suburb of Saint-Germain-en-Laye. And what's best, we could park wherever we wanted.

Well, that last bit wasn't strictly true. I've had it towed away twice for questionable parking efforts, but I've heard that's a pretty low score for a Parisian scooter. A French friend of mine put it this way: riding a scooter in Paris comes with a 120 euro annual parking permit. While it's technically free to park most places, you're pretty much guaranteed to get it towed every six months (with a 60 euro pick-up fee each time).

By my calculations, that was still wildly cheaper than an annual car park in a cramped city like Paris.

But the unexpected pleasure that came with the scooter was the act of driving in Paris. Sure, it was nice to be able to get to distant places and to park for only 120 euros a year. It was a treat to sleep in a few extra minutes on workdays too. But nothing compared to the feeling of seeing Paris from the middle of the roads. Surprisingly, it was right up there with riding through the French Riviera in a storm. You see, when you cycle in Paris you're typically hugging the kerb, hoping not to get hit by a bus, and trying to avoid wayward pedestrians. When you're driving a car or a truck you're forever bogged down by the traffic. But when you're on a scooter you become the king of the road. The other motorists respect you, for a reason I've never really understood. I sometimes wonder if it's because they feel guilty to be driving a big empty car when we're on little scooters. Maybe it's because they're terrified of knocking a scooterist off their bike. Who knows?

But the best bit is peeling away from the masses when the traffic light turns green. A scooter is much lighter than a car, so it can take off much, much faster. So when there was traffic at a red light, I could easily scoot up between all the stationary cars to the front. The motorists are usually excellent at leaving a lane between them for us bikers. And once at the front, when that light goes green, and when I've got a beautiful boulevard in front of me, then there's no place I'd rather be.

Funnily enough, the scooter revealed itself to be a real head turner on the streets of Paris too. Most of the city's scooters are nondescript, forgettable, and ugly. But not mine. Mine stood out like a gleaming little fire engine in a sea of black. Other scooterists would often turn to me at a red light and ask me where I got it from. Or how much it cost. Or they'd just say that it was beautiful. Once an elderly woman crossing the road in front of me turned and suggested I should work for the local fire station with colours so bright. And often, when I parked it outside of a cafe or restaurant, I'd watch people take photos of it - sometimes climbing aboard for the opportunity.

But the driving was the best bit. And if you'd like a tip for an enjoyable ride, I'd point you in the direction of the big boulevards, like Sebastopol on the Right Bank, where you can get from one end to the other catching every light the moment it turns green. The absolute best scooter drive in Paris, without a doubt, is Quai des Grands Augustins on the Left Bank, which runs west along the riverside and past all the famed monuments. If you ever have the chance, rent a scooter and drive it from Notre Dame to the Eiffel Tower and you'll see what I mean.

4.4 Finding our feet

There was something beautiful about getting to know Paris together with Lina, another foreigner in Paris. I often thought about this, actually, because a fair few of my foreigner friends had come to Paris for a French person. That French person could not only help them navigate the minefields of administration, but could also point out the best milk to buy, the best restaurants, the streets to avoid, and everything from Metro etiquette to language lessons.

I had none of those luxuries and neither did Lina. We were two foreigners in Paris; we were lost at sea but we were lost together. If you can imagine the romanticism of a weekend away with a loved one in Paris, exploring, taking wrong turns, laughing in strange restaurants... that had been us for almost two years, and we loved it. Making mistakes was one of the great pleasures of coming to understand Paris and it's something I'd encourage any tourist to do too.

But don't get me wrong, it's also hard. It takes time to learn the things we took for granted back home, like knowing which brand of yoghurt was best, or which telephone company had an awful reputation, or where you should never walk at night. These things we learned the hard way, or at least the long way.

I was also coming to appreciate the intricacies of Paris. I'd surprised myself, really. I was never a big fan of history or architecture, but life in the centre of Paris changed me dramatically. I found myself devouring the information plaques that crop up all over the city. I marvelled at the dramatic stories that have changed the face of Paris over the centuries. I loved how if you looked hard enough, you could find traces of history on the lampposts, the doors, the walls…

And while Lina and I still liked our little apartment, it came with a few annoyances too. I missed having proper showers, standing up straight and washing my hair. We had to crouch due to the slanting ceiling, while holding the shower head in one hand. Sometimes we found ourselves longing for an elevator, especially when returning from the supermarket. And what I really would have loved was a west-facing window in the bathroom or kitchen. That way, we would have had unspoiled views of the Eiffel Tower, which was still only visible from the communal toilet. Such a western view was impossible to even create, as the whole west-facing wall was blocked off by a huge unused chimney that ran along the building and extended high above our rooftop. If it weren't for that chimney, our view would have been twice as impressive. But instead, it felt like half the city was hidden from view because of a chimney. It was such a shame to think of what we were missing, and strange to consider that two years ago I'd been so smitten with the rooftop view to the south. But I'm a sucker for that Eiffel Tower and I wanted to be closer to it.

What I really needed, as you'll probably agree, was a little bit of perspective, thank you very much, and it would come in the most unexpected of ways.

4.5 Paris from the top

I was reminded of the beauty of Paris in a rather surprising way one autumn morning. Lina was out of town and I was home alone when there was a knock at the door. What with the often impenetrable front doors to Paris apartments, I knew that it was probably my neighbour Stephane. And I was right.

"Oliver, ze sun is shining, ze weazzer eez magnifique. I need someone to enjoy eet wizz. What are you doing?"

I was doing nothing and I told him so.

"Parfait, come wizz me. *Wino.*"

Ah, some things never change, I'd forever be a *"wino"* to Stephane. We crossed the corridor of the seventh floor landing and he led me to the far side of his equally small apartment.

"I 'ope you don't fear ice," he added, giving me a mischievous wink.

Ice? What tricks did Stephane have in mind? Gin and tonics on his balcony? Did he have a balcony...

Stephane launched open his window, which was the same style as my own - built into the sloping ceiling so he had to lift it upwards.

I'd never seen the view from his apartment, but because it was on the opposite side of the building it was quite different from mine. He had an eastern-facing window, which was pretty intriguing to me. I glanced out towards the Marais and the Bastille, getting my bearings. But that was nothing compared to what was coming.

"Well, nowz ze time to tell me. Do you fear ice?"

"Ice? No. Why would I fear ice?"

"*Non*, not ice, *ice!*" he said, pointing out the window and towards the ground.

I looked down at the courtyard seven floors below, then back at Stephane who was grinning madly as usual. Ice? *Ice?*

"You know, ice, when you are 'igh up in ze 'eavens."

"Oh *heights*!? You mean am I afraid of *heights*?" I said.

"Zat's exactly what I said, ice," Stephane said.

I laughed. It's true, the French don't care much for the letter H when speaking English. Except when there's a *silent* H. That's exactly when they often decide to pronounce it. I've heard a few Parisians say *'appy Hour* rather than *Happy 'our*.

"Don't laugh at me, or we will sweetch to français and eet will be me who eez laughing," Stephane said. "So, do you fear HHHeights or not?"

The truth is, I'm not afraid of heights at all. Or ice, incidentally. I grew up climbing trees like a jungle child. I've bungee jumped in three different continents. I've peered into the depths of the Grand Canyon and cleared snow from Swedish rooftops. But when I saw Stephane scramble through his window and out onto the sloping rooftop I almost wet myself. Was he crazy? It was a drop of seven floors. It was certain doom if he slipped. From out on the rooftop Stephane must have sensed my fear.

"Don't worry," he said. "Zairs a chimney blocking your fall. Eet's not as bad as eet looks."

I'm ashamed to admit it, and I know my own mother will never forgive me, but I caved in to the charming Frenchman and I climbed through the damn window. I didn't look down and I followed him up the sloping roof to the top, which came to an apex of death before sloping downwards on the other side. Stephane guided me to what he said was the best spot, the flat slab of concrete that held a dozen terracotta chimney pots in place. I climbed on top of it, and, for the first time, surveyed my surroundings.

I don't know if it was the fear of falling or the astonishing beauty of Paris, but when I looked around I could hardly breathe. It was immense. I was standing in the epicentre of the city and I could see uninterrupted in every direction. Better still, there wasn't a person in sight. The sensation was extra special because I was standing on top of my own building, where I'd lived for two years, and I was getting a sudden new perspective on it. Sacre-Coeur was shining in resplendent white to the far north, the Eiffel Tower gleaming away to the southwest. With just that added bit of height I could see so much further. I could see the skyscrapers in the suburbs, Notre Dame, the Pantheon, the spire of the Sainte Chapelle, the roof of the Opera, the looming Montparnasse tower, and everything in between.

I could also look down on my own bedroom window, which was an odd sensation in itself, and I could finally grasp just how close we were to having that uninterrupted Eiffel Tower view. The chimney blocking it was huge!

I also understood how much taller our apartment block was than the other ones around it. The buildings across much of Paris, especially in the centre, were typically built to a uniform shape and size thanks to the grand redesign of the city by Baron Haussmann in the 19th century. They're all six or seven floors and more or less equal in height. But we were higher, who knows why. I wasn't thinking about *that* at the time. I was thinking about the city. The sheer scale of it. And how fortunate I felt to be living in the middle.

Stephane took a great picture of me up there, standing among the chimney tops, with both arms outstretched to my sides. Behind me, Paris, with the spire and towers of Notre Dame visible below my right wrist. (The same spire that was to tragically burn to ashes just two years later.) Stephane's picture captured our little adventure perfectly. My whole body was full of energy, fear, and excitement. I was lucky to be alive, that was for sure. But I also realized that if I wanted to stay alive, I should get off the roof.

I climbed down and thanked Stephane for the invite. The experience was exhilarating, but I never went up there again. Paris is probably best enjoyed from the pavement, to be honest. But every now and again it's nice to see it from the top.

4.6 Leaving Montorgueil

Two people can live in a shoebox apartment for two years, and not a day more. That's the limit. This dawned on Lina and me one morning as if it were the most natural thought in the world. We figured that it would be mad to spend another day in that tiny *chambre de bonne*, so we went looking for something bigger. And like so many Paris apartment stories I've heard, we found our perfect place by pure chance.

We'd been invited to a party in the 11th arrondissement by a French drag queen we'd met somewhere along the way. The theme for the night: "Dress up in drag. Well, at least make an effort." The host added that no one should make *too much* of an effort because *she* wanted to look the best, of course. And perhaps surprisingly for a drag party, it wasn't the costumes that grabbed our attention. It was the apartment. It was breathtaking. It had an enormous living room with original fishbone parquet floors, ceiling-high windows, and double glass doors to the bedroom. At four floors up, it was just above the tree line and it had a charming view over the intersection of a quiet Parisian street and rue Charonne. After sufficient compliments to the host about her dress, makeup, and wig, we asked about the apartment.

"How on earth did you find this place, it's amazing," I said.

"Oh this old place? You like it? Well I love it too, darling, but I'm upsizing next month. If you want, I could get you ahead of the queue. We can put in a good word with the real estate agent. She's an old friend of my family. And don't tell anyone I told you, but you can get this place for a steal."

Lady Luck was showing her gorgeous face once more and I was ready to chase her. We said we were in. The drag queen winked one massive eyelash at me, said it would be done, then strode elegantly to the front door to greet some new arrivals. Lina and I couldn't believe our good fortune.

We met with the real estate agent, Madame Raymond, a few weeks later. She told us she couldn't speak a word of English, but that it didn't matter - there wouldn't be any need for lengthy discussion because this was an open and shut deal. The drag queen had put in a good word for us. All we had to do was confirm that we were happy with the place.

Madame Raymond took us into the apartment and flung open the front door. And if we'd thought it was brilliant during the evening, we weren't prepared for the sheer impressiveness of it in full daylight. Our eyes were met with an almost blinding natural light that swept the room. Being above the trees, with ceiling-high windows, and an unusually low building across the road, there was nothing to stop the light from flooding into the room and reflecting off the wooden floors.

It was so powerful, so beautiful, that I almost had to look away. And it seemed even bigger than we remembered, because the drag queen had moved out and taken the furniture. And of course, the room wasn't filled with big wigs and feather boas anymore either. We inspected the rest of the apartment, almost shivering with excitement that a place like this could be so affordable. We started talking about how our lives would change once more with the move, how we could finally have guests not only for dinner - but also for the weekend. Hell, we could even get furniture.

It all seemed too good to be true, just like my first place, which was starting to feel smaller and smaller by the minute.

"So, Madame Raymond, show me the dotted line," I said in English.

She didn't understand and I didn't know how to say the same thing in French, so I just said that it was perfect and that we would very much like to take it.

"*Fantastique*," she responded. "I'm sure you will love it here. Now, all we need is your *dossier* and the apartment is yours."

Ah, the *dossier*. I'd heard about the *dossier* before and hoped I'd never come face to face with someone who wanted one. My current landlady had never mentioned it. I'd never had to take the time to make one. Essentially, the *dossier* is a set of documents that proves you have a stable job with enough of a regular income to cover the rent. You have to prove that those living in the home earn three times the rent each month. Now, I wasn't earning that much money, but if you added my salary to Lina's - who had just started an independent shoe company - then we could scrape through. We went home and made our first *dossier*, crossing our fingers that we hadn't missed any details and that Madame Raymond wasn't showing the apartment to others. We sent it off before the end of the day on Friday, after translating a bunch of Lina's Swedish work documents into French for the benefit of the future landlord. The real estate agent said she would get back to us on Monday.

We spent the weekend planning the big move. For the first time, we found ourselves inspecting furniture in the flea markets - something we didn't have the luxury (or the space) for in the *chambre de bonne* apartment. We discussed how life was set to change. I almost sent a letter to my landlady saying that I was on the way out.

Luckily I didn't.

Because on Monday morning I got the bad news from Madame Raymond.

"You two seem so lovely, but I'm afraid we just can't let you have the apartment without a full *dossier*. You both need French jobs with French incomes. It's simply impossible. I'm sorry."

Heartbreak.

Well, the goddess of fortune is a fickle one, and I should have realized that going in. We had the money for the apartment, but not the paperwork. And we couldn't get the paperwork. The dream apartment went out the window and we were left with two options: 1) Get Lina a French job so we could have a French *dossier*. 2) Find an apartment through someone who doesn't care about *dossiers*.

It was only then, two years into my Parisian life, that I realized how lucky I'd been to find the *chambre de bonne* apartment we were living in. I have no idea why that landlady didn't want my papers. But now it seemed that we'd have to wait if we were going to move from our lovely little shoebox. It was a definite kick in the shins, French administration trying to have the last laugh; but as I've said before, the only way to beat French admin is to make sure you're laughing first.

Even if it's a bitter, dejected, and somewhat angry laugh.

CHAPTER FIVE

The Earful Tower and a
new French president.

5.1 The radio

Two years had passed since I moved to Paris and I was in a slump.
The news that I had come to cover was getting me down. There was
just so much horror, so much terror. Since I'd been in the Paris office
there'd been the Charlie Hebdo terror attack, the November attacks
at the Bataclan, the Bastille Day attack in Nice, plus a spate of other
terror-related shootings and stabbings, not to mention the horrific
Germanwings plane crash in the French Alps. News, by its very nature,
is often bad - and I was realizing that it wasn't giving me the Paris experience I'd been hoping for. But it wasn't just that. Working in a small
team in a startup meant a lot of work and not a lot of exploring Paris.
Being at the desk from 9-6, Monday to Friday, meant I never really
had my finger on the pulse of the city for anything besides its news. I

didn't know how busy a Paris cafe was at 2 pm on a Wednesday. I didn't know when the garbage men typically came down my street. I didn't know whether the Metro was busy outside of peak hour on a weekday.

It was around this point that we had a young intern at the news site, James, who was flat broke and looking for opportunities. He'd been with us a while and was eager to find a full time gig. One day, while scrolling around online, I saw a job as a junior producer on a radio station called World Radio Paris. I sent him the link, he applied for the job - and got it. Not long down the line, he got back in touch with me.

"Ollie, mate, if you're interested in hosting a radio show, I've got a volunteer spot for you," he said. "Have a think about it, and if it's something for you, come along to meet the other volunteers at the studio. Come and discover the truth."

The truth, huh? Bit strange, I thought. I did indeed consider it, but my instinct was telling me that it wasn't for me. I'd always been interested in radio, but this was sounding like more work; more news, more grim reporting. Many, if not most reporters out there were far more invested in journalism than I was, far more talented at it, and far more serious, living and breathing the news and discussing it outside of office hours. Not me. I enjoyed the news, but I didn't devour it in the way other journalists did. This made me hesitant to take on more reporting at the radio.

I should stress that my time at the news site was hugely memorable and important for me. While the editor may have been disappointed in my taste for raw bacon and the fact that I never got a French girlfriend, he was instrumental in teaching me so much of what I know about reporting. But not just that: he's the one who taught me what's important in France, which stories matter, what the readers care for (and why they care). He gave me the context I so sorely lacked when I had moved to France two years earlier. And he was an expert at looking through a French newspaper and knowing exactly which stories an international audience would want to read.

Despite my initial hesitation about the radio, I couldn't shake the idea of at least dipping my toe into that world. Just nothing newsy. Nothing too much like work. A kind of talk show, perhaps. A series of interviews with interesting people, talking about Paris. Why not? I texted the idea to James and he invited me to meet the other volunteers the next week. I listened in to the station in the following days and was impressed by the work the others had put in. There were music reviewers, interviews with artists, and people sharing their life stories about Paris. When I went to the meeting, everyone in the room explained their programmes and ideas to the group. They were all volunteers, fun-loving people. Making radio shows for the listeners out of the goodness of their hearts. They were a ragtag bunch, carefree, living for the joy of "on air" conversation.

When it was time to explain my idea, I told them how I wanted to escape the clutches of the news and do a talk show, and they all politely listened. The only thing they stressed was that if I wanted to join them, then it had to be for a full season. No dipping a toe in, I had to dive in headfirst. I nodded to show my understanding.

After the meeting, James took me aside. He could sense that I was hesitant to sign up as a volunteer, hesitant to commit to something for so long. We sat on two large leather armchairs and there was an unmistakable darkness that crept over the room as he made his pitch. He looked me in the eye.

"You're a slave, Oliver, working in a job that is prison for your mind," he said.

Bit harsh. But fair.

He explained that I *needed* to explore community radio, or, The Truth, as he called it.

"Unfortunately, no one can be told what community radio is. You have to see it for yourself. This is your last chance. After this there is no turning back."

Why did this sound so familiar? Where had I heard this? Was he quoting something?

He continued, leaning forward so that his leather trench coat creaked against the armchair.

"You say no - the story ends, you wake up in your bed and believe whatever you want to believe. You sign up as a volunteer - you stay in Wonderland, and I show you how deep the rabbit hole goes. Remember: all I'm offering is The Truth. Nothing more."

That's what this was. It was The Matrix, definitely The Matrix.

James, who had a penchant for theatrics, was having a Morpheus moment with me, offering me the proverbial blue or red pill to help stress the importance of the decision. Theatrics aside, James was right to take the matter seriously, as it was a choice that would eventually change my life. But I didn't know it at the time.

I told him I'd give him my answer in a week.

5.2 The Earful Tower

One night after a basketball game in the old marketplace sports hall, I went for a beer with two American musicians. Their names were Sam and Aurelien, and they had a band called Slim and the Beast. I told them my idea for a radio show. I told them that I had an open offer, but that I was still hesitating. And they didn't tolerate that.

"So you're saying you could do a radio show; you've got an idea; and you've got nothing to lose? What's stopping you?" asked Sam.

I listed a few concerns and Aurelien looked baffled.

"Who cares? Just do it."

"What if I can't find guests? What if every week I end up struggling to come up with ideas? Where would I even start?" I asked.

"We'll be your first guests, we'll bring the guitars," Sam said.

"Yeah, we're not even gonna discuss it anymore. When you come to basketball next week, come with a time and a date for episode one," Aurelien added.

One thing I admire about Americans is that they believe anything is possible. I've heard that American children grow up hearing that they can be president one day - and it instills confidence in them, for better or worse. These two Americans believed in me, and I needed that boost. So just like that, the idea was in place and I had my first guests. I confirmed my commitment with James, booked my first studio time and starting writing questions for the band. There was just one piece missing, I realized as my telephone beeped.

"Ollie, we need a name for your show." It was James, of course. And I had nothing for him.

I went for a walk along the Bassin de la Villette during my lunch break at the news site. The *bassin* is a big stretch of water that picks up where the Canal Saint-Martin stops off. And as I walked, I thought about my new show. How to sum up a radio show that's meant to be fun, entertaining, light - and, crucially, about Paris? I went through the main words associated with the city, as everyone who's ever written a book, a blog, or made a social media account about Paris has done before me. Baguette. Croissant. Cafe au lait. Vin rouge. Nope, nothing.

What about place names? Paris. Arc de Triomphe. Sacre-Coeur. Nothing still. I wandered up on a green iron bridge that crossed the water and saw, way off in the distance, the top floor of the Eiffel Tower. Funny, I thought, I'd been working right here for two years and I didn't know we had this view just outside. The Eiffel Tower was in my mind, on the tip of my tongue and I kept thinking about my show. How could I sum it up? Something to listen to, something to hear, something for your ears… Hang on, hang on… Something for your ears… something about the Eiffel Tower. Bullseye! "The Earful Tower." I felt a rush of excitement and I texted James immediately.

"The show will be called The Earful Tower," I wrote.

And so my next chapter began. The Earful Tower was born.

The early days of The Earful Tower were carefree and fun. The radio station had no accurate statistics for how many people listened - if anyone at all. I'd asked James to be my sidekick for the show, and as a thanks, I'd bring a bottle of red wine or two into the studio. And we'd fly by the seat of our pants every time.

The first-ever episode, as agreed with Sam and Aurelien, was with their band. They brought their guitars and harmonicas into the studio and I was so nervous that I'd planned out the half-hour interview to the minute. Even though I knew the guests (and perhaps because we had a glass or two of wine before we started), I felt like I had no idea what I was about to do. I had a list of questions, and James had time cards to let us know how long we'd been talking. And I was nervous. But as soon as we got going that night, the strangest thing happened. I felt a kind of calmness as we pressed "record". A serenity. Everything else faded away and I was truly present in the moment. Sure, I had the questions beside me, but I didn't need them. And sure, James would hold up a time card every five minutes, but I didn't really need that either. Whether that first episode was any good or not - you can be the judge. It's still out there, right at the bottom of the list. But something about it just felt right, and I was already craving more.

I reached out to a bunch of people I'd interviewed in the past for the news site. I'm amazed, looking back, that any of them agreed to be on my show. I can only imagine that it was a mix of my persistence, that they knew who I was from my journalist days, and that they were intrigued by radio.

But some of those early guests were big names in the Paris expat scene. There was acclaimed pastry chef and writer David Lebovitz, author Stephen Clarke, who I'd long admired before I ever moved to France, and there was the former head of the New York Times Paris bureau, Elaine Sciolino. I actually recorded with Elaine in the Shakespeare and Company bookshop after she'd given a talk, which was a wonderful treat in itself. But another fortuitous thing happened that night - I met another author, Australian John Baxter. He had been giving a talk with Elaine and I approached him afterwards. We chatted, ever so briefly, and ever so forgettably for him, I'm sure. I'd never have predicted that a year down the track we'd have become friends. And I certainly wouldn't have guessed that it'd be after his birthday party that I'd propose to Lina on a Parisian bridge. But I'm getting ahead of myself again.

I was meeting interesting people and I was loving it. It was fun too, despite the fact that the "studio" was just a desk in an open-plan office. The radio station had permission to use it after 7 pm, provided all the office workers had gone home for the day. It wasn't a professional setup, but they had great microphones and that's all we really needed. The dream, of course, was to have a private studio where we could record at any time of the day, and that was apparently in the pipeline, they said.

After a few months of the amateur hour on the radio, James told me that things were sailing smoothly.

"You know, there's a spike in traffic every time we air one of your shows," he said. "There could be something in this."

The head of the radio station contacted me to tell me the same thing.

"What do you know about podcasting?" he asked me.

"Absolutely nothing," I responded.

He explained that a podcast was just like a radio show, except subscribers could download it to their phone and enjoy it at their own leisure, rather than, say, every Friday at 8 pm like a radio programme.

It was all new to me. And little did I know that before long I'd be teaching podcasting at a Parisian university, meeting with mayors, and wrestling with crocodiles. But there I go again, getting *way* ahead of the story.

5.3 The eleventh

The hunt for a new apartment ended when a friend left Paris and leased us her apartment in the trendy 11th arrondissement. We ended up staying there for the next 18 months. The apartment was twice as big as the maid's quarters on the seventh floor, and half as charming. But our friend didn't need a *dossier*, just a promise that we'd pay rent. I handed in my notice for our tiny flat and we moved soon after. Two years in that minuscule place seemed ridiculous in retrospect, but I still don't regret it at all. In fact, I still miss it sometimes.

But life in the 11th was a whole new Paris. Gone were the tourists, for one thing. And it wasn't as picture perfect as the 2nd arrondissement, no sir. But it was interesting in another way. We lived on rue de la Fontaine au Roi - King's Fountain Road - which ran from the Canal Saint-Martin all the way up a gently sloping hill into Belleville. The street was named after the fountain that once provided Parisians with water, which ran through aqueducts to the town below. The fountain is long gone now and the street is perhaps better known nowadays for housing one of the bars that was targeted in the terror attacks. It was no coincidence that those terrorists had chosen the 11th district to attack, because the terraces of the local bars were always full.

But it was a pretty fascinating place to live, especially in those days. Gentrification was sweeping up our street like an Australian bushfire, and taking everything in its path. We watched it happen right outside our front door. When we moved in, there was an ageing internet cafe across the road. Within months, it was replaced by an organic fruit and vegetable shop, then a hipster Asian restaurant. The shops on both sides of it had similar fates. Senegalese restaurants turned into specialty coffee shops. A nearby bar that was once popular with elderly locals turned into the hippest dive bar in the neighbourhood. But not everyone was thrilled with the new face of the 11th arrondissement. On the local bistro-turned-dive-bar, someone took a black marker pen and scrawled in big, English letters on an outside wall: Hipsters Die!

Our 18 months in the area included a lot of socializing, particularly around the Canal Saint-Martin, the city's picnicking capital. Our timing was perfect, our neighbours said. The canal area had only recently undergone a facelift that saw hipsters replace drug dealers, and cafes in the place of tired shops. As for us, we'd sit on the canalside with a bottle of wine from a nearby supermarket and stay long into the night. If it got cold we'd wander into one of the nearby bars or restaurants, or we'd migrate gradually uphill to the happy hours of rue Saint Maur and beyond. Over the two years we'd been in Paris we'd surrounded ourselves with a good group of friends, and we rarely stayed home when the weather was good.

And it wasn't only that we had more friends. We noticed that living on the ground floor made it a whole lot easier to duck out onto the street - for whatever reason. I found myself popping out for ingredients as Lina had developed a keen interest in baking, thanks to the fact that we finally had a real oven after two years without one. Lina was baking like a woman possessed and her cakes and muffins were delicious. And I could run out and get eggs within three minutes. It was wonderful. But the best part of it all, we agreed, was finally escaping the seven flights of stairs (with no elevator) which had eventually made it a chore to leave the flat.

Back in those early days in the 11th, I remember we once sat down over a fresh banana cake - Lina's new speciality - to toast to the new lives ahead of us and the new opportunities. We tried to figure out just how many times we had climbed up the dreaded 118 stairs in the 2nd arrondissement. And we vowed never to live on the top floor of a walk-up again. At that precise moment, I got a text from James at the radio station.

"Good news, *mec*, they've signed the lease on a new studio, we've got it all to ourselves. We can record at any time of the day or night. It's a bright new future and a bright new studio," he wrote. "PS: It's on the sixth floor (with no elevator)."

Ah, some things never change.

5.4 The resignation

It's a strange thing to be recognized by your voice. I'd been running The Earful Tower for six months and I felt I was on to something. People were writing in from around the world to say they were listening. Friends, who had gone beyond the stages of listening to support me, surprised me by discussing recent episodes. The momentum was thrilling. One day I was at Le Peloton cafe in the Marais and I was ordering drinks at the counter. As I headed out to a table on the terrace, a man stopped me in my tracks.

"Oliver?" he said with a start. "Oliver Gee?!"

He wasn't asking it, he was exclaiming it. He was almost jittery with excitement.

"Yep, that's me…." I said.

"No way!" he continued. "I thought it was you! I recognized your voice when you ordered the coffees."

Then he sang the jingle that I had been using in the early episodes, composed on the spot by Slim and the Beast.

"The Earful Tower, with Oliver Geeeee," he sang, turning back to his friends with his eyes wide. "This guy does that podcast I was telling you about. Remember?"

The jingle bit was slightly embarrassing. More embarrassing was the fact that his friends apparently had no idea what he was talking about. They gave polite nods. I blushed and thanked him for listening, then headed to the outside terrace with our coffees. I was with Lina and a friend and they thought it was a hoot. As we sat down, they were laughing and punching me in the arm. Fancy getting recognized by your voice, they said. But then it got even weirder. Only two minutes had passed when an American woman came running down the street.

"Oh my gawd, you're Oliver Gee. I can't believe it!"

She'd recognized my face from a video I'd done and said she'd come to the cafe because I'd mentioned it on the show. In fact, she'd taken a lot my recommendations, it turned out.

"Oh my lawd, I love it. I love it! What a scream! And I've gotta tell ya, I've taken all your tips and I've done them all," she said, reeling off the tours she had taken, the restaurants she'd visited, and the books she had bought - all based on the guests from my show.

"D'ya mind if I have a picture with you?" she asked.

It was flattering to know that my work had such an effect on someone's holiday. But I also got a little niggling feeling of something else. What was it? Ah, that's it. Missed opportunity. That was the day that I realized that there was a real potential in the show. That was the day that it dawned on me that people were not just passively listening, they were *actively* listening. They were using the show for insights into Paris. And perhaps most importantly, they were spending money. Not on me, mind you. But surely there was a way I could twist this thing so I was getting a slice of the pie too. The almost tangible scent of opportunity was so strong that before I had figured out how to mone-tize my show, I handed in my resignation at the news site.

Let's be totally honest here, it wasn't just that sense of opportunity that made me quit the job. It was also time to go. You know when you're reading a book and your mind wanders elsewhere, then suddenly you snap back and wonder how much you've missed? Well that's a little how I felt with my job. And I couldn't figure out how long I'd been looking at the words without taking them in. It was time to snap out of it.

I'd love to say that quitting my job was a brilliant move and that from that moment on I became rich, but that's not true at all. It was a move that, practically at least, was quite stupid. Many French people told me afterwards that the trick is to negotiate when you quit; leave on good terms, and then you'll continue to earn a large portion of your salary from the state. It's called a *rupture conventionelle*, in case you're ever planning to do the same. But I didn't do it. No, not me. Not foolish old Oliver. I could sense the new energy in the Paris air and I wanted to drink it, to breathe it in, to live it. Exactly *how* I'd make money from a podcast didn't enter my mind at all; I just knew I could do it.

I was 30 years old and I figured I was still young enough to strug-gle on a new project. I gave a month's notice to my editor, meaning my last day would be right after the French presidential election of 2017. After more than two years working as a full-time reporter in Paris, my stint with the news site was going to end with a big story.

5.5 Le Président de la République

After five years working at the news site (including three in Stockholm, but that's for another book) my time as a journalist was coming to an end. The French were deciding whether to vote in their youngest leader since Napoleon, Emmanuel Macron, or Marine Le Pen and the far right. The election was to be my last story for the news site which seemed to be a fitting book end.

In the lead-up we reported the hell out of that election, and I'm glad to say that by now my French was much improved. I travelled around Paris and France and listened to anyone who'd talk. I spoke to young Parisians who were excited by the prospect of a president in his thirties. I went to a National Front rally in a former coal mining town, Hénin-Beaumont, where Marine Le Pen was a hero and people were hoping her anti-EU, anti-immigrant policies would turn their lives around. I even went to ghost towns in rural France where no one cared who would win and no one cared to even vote. In Roubaix, which was once the beating heart of the textile industry, people were so disenchanted with it all that they didn't even want to talk to me about the election. The French papers called it the "capital of abstention" after 45 percent of people didn't bother voting the last time around. It was fascinating to see how France could be so divided. Walking the streets of the towns in northern France made it evident, once again, that Paris wasn't France and France wasn't Paris. But no matter which way the vote went, France was going to get a change, which was clearly what everyone was after.

On the night of the election I was sent to the courtyard of the Louvre museum, where Macron accepted his victory. He strode out to greet the crowds as the European anthem, Beethoven's Ode to Joy, blared from nearby speakers. He'd won in a landslide: 66 percent of the vote, and as I stood among the crowd of thousands, the result seemed to me like the exact kind of news that France needed. A fresh start. New ideas. And a pretty clear "*non, merci*" to Marine Le Pen.

I stumbled home that night exhausted, but relieved to have finished my work with the news site on a high after two years that included a lot of heavy reporting. But it felt like good news that night: the energy in the young crowd at the Louvre was exhilarating and contagious. They were excited for something new and so was I. But my new chapter had nothing to do with Macron. I was going to tell my own story.

I took a break after the election and spent some time setting up The Earful Tower to be its own entity as a podcast. I taught myself how to edit audio files so that I didn't need to rely on any outside help to produce the episodes. I built a website so I could see where the readers (and therefore the listeners) were. I joined a hosting platform to store all the episodes and launched social media pages. All these things I did organically, setting them up as I figured out that they were necessary. A long way down the road I learned that many new podcasters get weighed down by being prepared for "launch day", but it was never like that for me. When I realized I had an audience, I turned the radio show into a podcast. When I saw people wanted to follow me, I set up a Facebook page. When people starting asking for details of the next episodes, I decided to release them every Monday. It was all quite natural, I didn't plan it. But now that I was going to try and "make it" as a podcaster, I realized I needed to take it pretty seriously. This was going to be a bumpy ride, and I needed to be ready for it.

5.6 The U.S.

Quitting a full time job is a life-changing moment and should be celebrated accordingly. At least that's what I think. A sensible person would knuckle down and find a new job. An even more sensible person would have a new job to seamlessly switch to, preferably with a higher salary.

But someone like me thinks that quitting a job to pursue a podcast with no hint of an income should be celebrated.

So with this in mind, I bought a pair of one-way tickets to New York as a surprise for Lina. We spent the next six weeks in a rental car, driving from New York to Los Angeles, from where we'd eventually fly back to Paris. We took the back roads, saw some of the most famous places in the entire world, and it was fantastic.

Now I'd love to get into all the details of this road trip, but I don't think I should because 1) this is meant to be a book about France; and 2) there's a full chapter about a French road trip coming up soon. But believe me, that American journey was beyond a highlight. I think a lot of people who take similar holidays probably take Route 66 or something similar, and drive fairly directly between the two coasts - but not us. We first drove from New York to New Orleans - which, whenever I tell Americans, always prompts them to react the same way. *You went that far down?* We sure did. And it was crazier still. In case you know the United States well, here are the outliers on the map so you can connect the dots. New York, Atlanta, Memphis, New Orleans, Albuquerque, Kansas (yes, back through Texas), Las Vegas, San Francisco, then L.A. If you mapped out our journey it looks a lot less like a Route 66 cross section and more like a monitor for an arrhythmic heart.

But oh how wonderful it was! Especially the bits that were off the tourist trail. Sure, Nashville, the Grand Canyon, Hollywood, and Monument Valley are sublime. But I think my memories will always go back to the people. I'll remember the little basketball museum in rural Texas where I signed a ball for the owner, who thought I was a big-shot hooper from Australia. I'll remember being warned about returning to the town of Alligator, Mississippi because "folks go missin' in Alligator", at least according to the woman at the catfish restaurant in the next town. I'll remember one of our hosts telling us he was "an illegal drug dealer" before taking us two-step dancing in a small town in the South. And I'll remember the high school principal in Ness City, Kansas who wrote us into his weekly newsletter after we stopped into his school.

We covered 7,000 miles in six weeks and I had a newfound taste for big road trips. Luckily Lina did too. That adventure was over far too quickly for my liking, and I returned to Paris broke (again), but refreshed and ready to make a serious effort at podcasting. It was the first time in two and a half years that I was free in Paris. Remember, I didn't really know how Paris worked. Sure, I'd been free at the weekends and at the end of the work days. But what happens in the centre of the city at 10 am on a Tuesday? Are the bakeries busy on Thursday afternoons? Are waiters friendlier during off-peak hours? And how hard is it to get a seat on the terrace in the middle of the day?

These were the questions I wanted to answer. Weekends in Paris are chaotic and I now know they're not representative of the city in general. But weekends was all I'd had at this point. And I had been dreading the thought of one day leaving Paris and realizing that I only knew daily life from the weekends. So when we got back from the US and settled once more into Paris, I was giddy with excitement about exploring this second coming in the French capital.

CHAPTER SIX

———

Chasing crocodiles,
understanding cheese, and
making a viral video.

6.1 Live shows

I was very hungry as I approached 18 rue de l'Odeon, but as Ernest
Hemingway said in *A Moveable Feast,* you can enjoy Paris more when
you're hungry. He said the hunger made you appreciate the art, as if
you could feel the same hunger the artists were feeling when they were
working. But in my own hunger, Paris looked the same to me. All I
could think about was how I needed some food, and how I needed
some money to buy food, and how I needed a way to make money.

My first money-making scheme was to experiment with live
shows in Paris, with a paying crowd and an entertaining guest. And my
first target was John Baxter, an Australian author who'd been living in

Paris for decades and could tell a story better than just about anyone I knew. He'd invited me to discuss my plan at his apartment on the Left Bank, which had sweeping views over the city from the Notre Dame cathedral to Sacre-Coeur.

When Baxter opened the door I let it slip that I was hungry. In fact, I didn't let it slip. I asked him if he had anything to eat. Forget Hemingway and his romanticism, I needed a little morsel of something, even a piece of bread. Baxter, something of a chef on the side, took pity on my Oliver Twist routine and rustled up a quick feast; and then we got to talking. I say we got to talking, it was more just him talking, but that was fine by me. He was much more interesting than me and I was happy to listen. He told tales of his travels, his books, his lovers, and Paris. And I gobbled it up. This was the Paris I wanted to experience: chewing the fat with a prolific author on his balcony overlooking Paris. Eventually he asked what I had planned for the live show and I managed to convince him to be my guest. He had already been on my podcast and said he wanted to see it succeed, adding that he didn't expect a cut of any of the profits from tickets. I'd already arranged a venue for the show, down at the headquarters of a tour company by Notre Dame, nestled on the riverbank somewhere between the Tour d'Argent restaurant and the Shakespeare and Company bookshop.

Baxter told me that Sylvia Beach, who started the original Shakespeare and Company bookshop, had once lived in his apartment block, and that Hemingway would often come to visit her. I went home and skimmed through *A Moveable Feast* - and marvelled to see that I'd been walking the same steps as Hemingway that day. The only difference was that a hungry Hemingway refused the food and I asked for it.

So, here it was, a live show. My first real money-making plan since I quit my full-time job. I could sell tickets. Imagine if I could sell tickets for 20 euros. And imagine if I sold 50 of them. Would it be possible? That'd be 1,000 euros. Now, with 1,000 euros coming in I could surely buy some nice food and drinks for the guests, right? It was strange to think that 1,000 euros could be so exciting considering I'd been earning much more than that at the news site - but this would be my own earnings, all from my own ideas, something out of nothing.

Empowered by this wild scheme, I forgot one crucial aspect of the event planning. Twenty euros is a lot of money to spend to watch someone talk. Heck, for 20 euros you could get tickets to see the top athletes in the world perform in front of a sold-out arena. So why would you want to see me and John Baxter talking about Paris, even if there was a glass of champagne thrown in? Perhaps predictably for anyone besides me, tickets were slow to sell. In fact, they hardly sold at all. I emailed all my friends and acquaintances, but the sales dribbled in at best. Eventually, I realized that it would never sell out; I was far too small a voice on the Paris scene to gather a paying crowd. But just as I was about to invite everyone to come for free, thinking that a non-paying crowd is better than no crowd, I got an unexpected email from a lady in Dallas.

"Hi Oliver, I heard you're having trouble selling tickets to your show. Well, I love The Earful Tower, and if you promise to make a recording of the evening then I will buy a ticket and donate it to anyone in Paris who wants to come."

What an inspiring email! I was ecstatic. It never occurred to me that I could sell tickets to people who couldn't physically be there. The weight of imminent failure was lifted off my shoulders and I set about emailing listeners abroad who I knew loved the show. I told them that if they wanted to donate a ticket I would be happy to record the chat with Baxter. And those lovely listeners responded. One of them bought five tickets!

When the day for the show rolled around, I'd sold 40 tickets, mostly to people who'd never make it to the event and who had no intention to. I gave the spots away to anyone who wanted them, and would you believe it, 40 people crammed into the little room to watch the show. Those who got donated tickets brought treats from home and an Australian mate of mine, Mike, even baked cakes. The owners of the venue managed to sell drinks to guests, Baxter sold a few books, and everyone was happy. The show itself was a hit and Baxter was in fine form. It was lucky he'd said he didn't want a cut of the profits because there weren't many - not after the food and champagne I'd bought. With a belly full of (admittedly cheap) champagne and finger foods, I wasn't hungry anymore. At least not for food. But I *was* hungry to see where I could take the show. If I could sell tickets to a Paris event to people in Dallas, then surely there was a way to make this podcast succeed.

6.2 The crocodiles

You might know the Canal Saint-Martin from the stone-skimming scene in the hugely popular movie, *Amélie*. Or you might be familiar with it as a popular Paris hangout for youngsters and hipsters. But did you know there's at least one massive beaver in there? I swear it's true, I saw it with my own eyes. In fact, a group of us saw it swimming along without a care in the world. I was beside myself with excitement, running along the canal like an excited dog.

Now, the reason I cared so much about this beaver is because I'm Australian. One of the things I miss the most about Australia, by far, is the wild animals. Where I lived in Perth it wasn't unusual to see birds, tortoises, lizards, or snakes. Travel a little further out of the city and you'd see more kangaroos than you could imagine, plus emus, sharks, seals, dolphins, stingrays, and even penguins. In Paris, all I got was rats, which I quite liked to watch, to Lina's disgust. So after years of only rats and domesticated dogs, imagine the thrill of seeing a real live beaver, which was as exotic to me as a kangaroo was to a Parisian. I told a few people in the following days about the beaver sighting and they all scoffed. A beaver in the canal? Impossible. I researched the mysterious animal and found that it was most likely a coypu, which is basically as close to a beaver as you can get without being a beaver - just add a rat tail and you've got it. But what intrigued me far, far more than the beaver was the idea people were so adamantly against the notion of any animal living in the canal. It was so puzzling to me and made me want to dig deeper. The whole thing had an almost conspiratorial edge to it. What was the canal really hiding?

I told the story to a British videomaker and let him know how everyone doubted it. His eyes lit up. He'd also been itching to tell a story, to uncover a secret of Paris, so we set our minds to figuring out exactly what this mysterious creature could have been. We went down to the canal to interview some locals about whether they'd seen the beaver, or indeed whether they believed in it. Most people laughed it off. One, rather worryingly, said he'd heard council workers had recently found a body at the bottom of the canal, though that turned out to be wrong. One thing was clear, no one had seen the beaver and we seemed no closer to an answer - until the last interview of the day blew the entire story out of the water. I came across an elderly lady who was sitting on a bench by the canal, looking wistfully over the water. I didn't mention the beaver at first, and recorded our conversation about the canal. She said she liked to just sit there and watch the water, something I could relate to all too well.

Eventually, I turned to the subject to animals. Did she think, perhaps, that any creatures could live in the canal?

"But of course," she said. "There are birds, fish…" She looked out to the water again, a mischievous twinkle in her eyes.

"Do you think there could be… *beavers*?" I probed, holding my microphone ever closer.

"Why, yes of course. That wouldn't be surprising to me at all," she said, then paused, and looked straight into my very soul. I know there can't really have been a fire in her eyes, that would be impossible, but I swear I saw some kind of flame. She added:

"There are crocodiles in there too."

Crocodiles?! Did she say crocodiles? I almost laughed. At first I thought she had mistranslated the word crocodile. Maybe she meant lizard. But the word was the same in both languages. How could she know there were crocodiles in the Canal Saint-Martin? The woman wasn't anywhere near laughing, she was deadly serious.

"I know there are crocodiles, because I put them there."

Yep, she was serious. I had a hundred questions and I asked them all. I've listened to the full recording of our conversation and my tone changes gradually from sheer incredulousness to astonishment to baffled intrigue.

The lady said she'd had two pet crocodiles and had decided to release them into the canal for a better life. She'd done it a year earlier, after council workers had emptied and dredged the canal - as they do every 15 years or so. In other words, if the lady was telling the truth, and I honestly believed she was, then perhaps the crocs could go undiscovered for years.

Of course, the crocodile claim changed the whole plot of our beaver story. In fact, the beaver angle went out the window. I followed the crocodile trail instead, which led me to the mayor of the fourth arrondissement, who told me the tale of another famous crocodile discovered in the Paris sewers in the mid-1980s. That croc was captured by firefighters and sent to an aquarium in the French countryside. That part was true, I found the old news stories to prove it. But at this point, I was far more interested in the new crocs, and whether they could possibly survive in the murky depths of Paris. A marine biologist told me he was confident that if they indeed existed, two young crocodiles could thrive in such conditions. Imagine, he said, if it was a male and female. They could become a mating pair. He said young crocs like that would grow quickly, and could already be a metre long with an appetite for rats. Or beavers...

I honestly hope the story is true and that there *are* two growing crocs lurking in the Paris canals. I've always thought the canal needed a little extra something to liven it up, and two crocodiles would certainly do the trick. The hipster Parisians wouldn't be so quick to dip their toes in the water, now, would they?

I liked the story of the crocodiles so much that when we'd finished with all the interviews, we put it together as a podcast episode and performed it live in Paris. I rented a big room in a canal-side bar and invited a crowd to hear a "monstrously" good story. That was all I told them; I didn't want to give away any of the plot details. This time I charged 10 euros per ticket and around 70 people showed up. But that story had a longer tail than the rest of them. For months afterwards I got emails from people saying they couldn't look at the canal the same way. A year later a tour guide stopped me in the street to thank me for his go-to canal story for tourists. The Paris crocodiles made it to national radio in Australia and the pages of a book about Paris.

As for me, that crocodile story became one of my favourites, but it also taught me something valuable. While Paris is overflowing with some excellent tales from the history books, there are also plenty of new stories yet to be told. You've just gotta ask the right questions to find them.

6.3 Le Peloton Café

Where would a young Hemingway hang out if he was in Paris today? I often wonder. If you read his books about Paris, you'll see he spent a lot of time at what are now the famous cafes on the Left Bank. These places have become so popular, so touristy, so expensive, I feel like there's no way Hemingway would have ever stepped foot in them today. You know, I doubt he'd have even been on the Left Bank at all if he was down and out in Paris nowadays. So where would he be? If I had to guess I'd say the 11th arrondissement. Maybe the up-and-coming 19th or 20th. He probably wouldn't even be in Paris, more likely in a nondescript French town where accommodation is affordable and beers are cheap.

As for me, I realized I was inadvertently following in Hemingway's footsteps once again. Just like he did, I had quit my paying journalism job and was trying to make it on my own in Paris. But one thing was missing - I didn't yet have a regular cafe of my own.

Mine turned out to be Le Peloton, a spot opened by a pair of Anglophone expats, Paul and Christian, who were looking for a finishing point for their popular bike tours. I can't remember how I found the cafe, but I remember why I came back. It had everything I was looking for; a great location by the Seine River that wasn't far from my basketball court, English-speaking staff and customers, and good coffee. It was around a 30-minute walk from my apartment, something I also liked, as I remained a big fan of the aimless walk in Paris.

But there was one big problem. I still had essentially no income, and the coffees were €4 a hit. A struggling podcaster can't hole up in the corner of a cafe with those prices. The brainwave came - as most of my Paris brainwaves apparently do - over a canal-side picnic with the cafe owners, who were halfway through one of Lina's banana bread cakes. What if we could organize a barter system: one of Lina's cakes in return for free coffee? We agreed that every time Lina brought in a banana bread, they'd give us 10 coffees. And what do you know, the bread sold like hot cakes, so Lina kept making it. At one point the cafe owed us 80 coffees. For the price of a few bananas, sugar, and flour, Lina and I had a regular coffee shop hangout, and I had a working space. It was at Le Peloton that I'd have meetings, edit podcast episodes, or just enjoy some downtime. I was no stranger to sharing that information on the podcast - and it turned out people were listening.

One day I was sitting at the counter of the cafe when a tourist walked in, scouting the room with wide eyes. I heard her say "red scooter" to one of the owners, then watched as he pointed towards me. The woman approached, sidled up next to me at the bar, and said:

"I'd hoped you'd be here."

It took me by surprise. Who was this woman and what did she want from me? She continued.

"I've listened to every single episode of your show and I've been to this cafe twice hoping to meet you."

We got chatting and she revealed that she'd planned her vacation in Paris around the podcast. She knew *my* Paris, had eaten where I recommended, visited my favourite sites, and done walking tours with the guides I'd had on the show. She added that she was leaving the next day, and had done everything on her bucket list. All but one thing, it turned out, one burning question that remained. She lowered her voice.

"So, you have to tell me… was the crocodile story true?"

I told her that I believed it was true. Her eyes lit up.

"Well that's the one thing I haven't done. I want to explore the Canal Saint-Martin; I wanna find the crocodiles," she said.

Without a second's thought, I said I'd show her the canal right then if she'd like to book one of my walking tours. I had no idea why I said that, as I didn't do walking tours. I'd never given a walking tour before. She asked how much I charged. My mind raced. How much *did* I charge? Out of nowhere, I said 100 euros.

"Will you show me where the crocodiles were released?" she asked, tentatively.

Was she kidding? For 100 euros I'd have dived in to find them.

I'd never have guessed it, but as we walked towards the canal together, a crisp 100 euro note in my pocket, I realized I'd found another way to monetize the podcast. As the summer rolled around I found that there were more tourists who wanted to see my Paris, which was incredibly flattering. It wasn't really something I advertised - I didn't want to be a tour guide, after all - but when people came looking for it I was ready with a plan and a price. I developed a circuit around the Marais and the canal, where I'd tell the stories behind my shows. The places I found interesting in Paris. The kinds of places you could find crocodiles, if you believed those kinds of stories.

6.4 Finding Mary

I suppose now is as good a time as any to tell the story of when I first came to Paris. I was in my early 20s and had been travelling through eastern Africa. I was living on the tightest of tight budgets - and I arrived in London with just 20 pounds in my wallet. The rest of my family got to London at around the same time as I did for a big family reunion a few days down the line, and it was decided that I should take my little brother Eddie to Paris. He'd been learning all about the City of Light at school and was desperate to see it with his own eyes. I was hesitant at first. You see, he was 12 years old at the time, a young 12 by all means, and I was 21. I have no idea why anyone thought it was a good idea to leave Eddie in my hands, but that's what they did. With the Eurostar train far too expensive for our last-minute trip, we booked an overnight bus, packed a change of clothes, and arranged a bus ticket back a day later. All we'd need to do was find a place to stay overnight.

Before we left, my Dad took me aside, gripped me by the arm, and warned me to take good care of my brother. Yeah, yeah, I said. Let's go.

We got into Paris on a sunny summer afternoon and it was like a dream. Now I don't know what your first ever day in Paris was like - or maybe what it *will* be like - but ours was glorious and overwhelming at once. We got off the bus from London and hit the ground running. We walked until our feet were too sore to continue. We wanted to take it all in. Eddie, loveable Eddie, was beside himself with excitement and so was I, drinking it all up like a *chocolat chaud*.

"Look!" he said to me as we strolled by the River Seine. "Is that the Eiffel Tower?"

"Why, yes Eddie, I believe it is," I said with a smile and ruffled his hair.

"Boy oh boy, it's a lot bigger than in my school books," he said. "Can we go and see it?"

"All in good time," I responded. "First we need to find a tourism office and sort out a place for tonight. We need to sleep somewhere, after all," I said.

"Of course, Oliver, you know what's best," he said, flashing a cherub smile that showed his double dimple.

Now I was no expert on Paris in those days, but I knew we were near the most beautiful avenue in the world, the Champs-Elysées, and I figured there'd have to be some tourist help there. Plus I was keen to relax; I was surprised at how daunting the city was, the avenues so grand that it took an hour to walk along just one.

We crossed the elegant park, the Jardin des Tuileries, and made a beeline towards the Arc de Triomphe. About halfway along we discovered a little pop-up tourist booth, which looked like it could provide the answer to our questions of accommodation for the night.

It was here that I'd meet Mary, a curly-haired middle-aged French woman who didn't seem too impressed with me. I told her we were looking for a place to stay and she seemed incredulous. She asked how old Eddie was and I said 12. She asked if we had a signed document proving I was his guardian and I said no. She asked why I hadn't booked something ahead considering it was peak tourist season. I didn't have an answer. Mary didn't look impressed.

"It's the middle of summer, your brother is underage, you don't have a signed document from your parents saying that you're his guardian," she summarized. Then she shrugged her shoulders and added: "I suggest you find a park bench for the night."

Mary wasn't kidding. It was my first true encounter with a French person and I'm ashamed to admit that, like many other tourists, I decided that the stereotype was true. French people *were* rude, after all. We left Mary in the booth and went to sit on a nearby bench. I needed time to think and I wondered if we could sleep on a bench, really. I wondered how my parents would react. My Dad's warning played back in my mind: "Look after your brother". I felt I'd already let him down. I wondered how Eddie would react. I looked at his little 12-year-old face. His freckled cheeks. His tired and hopeful eyes.

"Are we really going to sleep on the bench, Ol?" he asked, using the nickname that only my closest friends and family ever use, especially in times of tenderness or trouble. "I'll do it if you ask me, you know what's best for me after all."

By God, that boy knew how to make me feel guilty.

"Don't worry, Eddie, I'll figure out something," I said. "You just lay down on the bench there and rest those sleepy little eyes."

While I waited to see if Eddie would fall asleep, I went through all my options. Now it might not sound like such a tricky situation to you, but let's get this in perspective. It was apparently forbidden to stay anywhere with Eddie without the legal consent from my parents, which I wasn't going to get. They were off in Morocco celebrating their wedding anniversary. I couldn't call them - none of us had cell phones, at that time and the internet wasn't even a remote possibility (for us, or for them!). I thought about forging something but then remembered that everything was apparently booked. Everything cheap, anyway, and I certainly couldn't afford anything expensive. And no, I couldn't whip out a credit card because I didn't have one - and Eddie didn't either. Nowadays it would be easy, I'm sure. But at that moment I didn't know what to do.

I looked over at Eddie, laying on the green bench, dozing off as the last rays of sunlight filtered through the Arc de Triomphe in the distance. I thought of my parents and how disappointed they'd be with me for making Eddie sleep on a bench. Night was starting to set in and there was a rat-like rustle coming from a nearby bush. Several rat-like rustles, in fact. I was astonished to see the first rat, poking its head out of the foliage and apparently sizing up Eddie's ankle - then retreating to wait for nightfall. I don't know what prompted my next act, and it may well have been the rats, but I gave up. I went back to Mary at the booth and brought Eddie along.

"Eddie, we have two options," I said before we approached. "Option one: you turn those doe-eyes up a notch and we charm this lady into helping us somehow. I don't know what she can do, but she's our only hope."

"And what's option two, Ol?" he said, his lip quivering.

"We sleep on the bench and get eaten alive by the Paris street rats."

We went back to the booth and I went through the options again. And to my dismay, Mary made it all sound even harder than she had at first.

After I'd all but exhausted my list of questions, I asked the last one I had.

"What would you do if you were me?"

She looked at Eddie, sweet Eddie, with dirt on his cheeks and what appeared to be a tear in his eye.

"How old is the boy again?"

"The boy is 12," I said. "And a young 12 at that."

She looked from Eddie to me and then back to Eddie again. She sighed. It was a long sigh. Then there was a long pause. Time stood still. It felt like the traffic on the Champs-Elysées disappeared. It was just me and Eddie and Mary as she decided what to tell us. It felt like she had the keys to the city, the insight, the context. Whatever she would say next would be our fate - and I was hoping she wouldn't repeat her line about the park bench. The sun had set by this point and Eddie, my beloved little brother, let out a little shiver. I put my arm around him.

I feel like it might have been that little shiver that changed everything, creating ripples that radiated despair and hopelessness through the air, reaching Mary and warming up her Parisian heart.

"*Alors*," she said, shaking her head. "My son is 12 and I wouldn't want him sleeping on a bench in Paris." Another pause. "I suppose you two will have to sleep at my house. Come along, I'm closing up anyway."

What? Her house? Good lord, what a gesture! Here I was thinking she had some connection with a hotel or backpackers and would put in a good word for us. We couldn't believe our luck. Mary, who at first had seemed like the most heartless woman in Paris, had transformed into our guardian angel. She locked up the tourist booth and led us through the cobbled roads of the 8th arrondissement. We rode a train to the western suburbs, where we spent the night with Mary and her lovely family, in their wonderful home overlooking Paris. Her husband was delighted to meet two Australians, and we traded stories about life on our respective sides of the world. The 12-year-old French boy gave Eddie comic books while I drank wine with the adults. We got a true insight into Parisian family life, maybe better than any I've had in the years that I've lived here since.

In the morning, Mary sat down with us and pulled out a map of the city.

"Now, you've only got one day here so here's how to spend it," she said, marking with a pen the exact routes we should take and the sites we should see to maximise our time.

It was clear that this was her job, and she knew all the secrets. It was the perfect mix of tourist attractions and hidden gems. She told us how to avoid the queues at the Eiffel Tower and the best *bateau mouche* barge from which to see the city. And as a last surprise, she took us to the local bakery and plied us with pastry treats to take with us, then sent us on our way. It was amazing: we were well fed, well rested, and had the itinerary of an expert to lead us on our way. And so that second day was even more wonderful than the first. It was like a movie montage, with Eddie and I ducking and diving, smiling and laughing, riding boats and climbing towers until it was time to head back to London, drunk on the magic of Paris.

It was to be my first lesson in Paris know-how. Mary taught me that Paris doesn't have to be daunting and unmanageable. All you need is a few tips (and a place to sleep, of course). Funnily enough, years later, giving tips about Paris and helping tourists ended up being my own job. I sometimes wonder if I'll pay back the accommodation favour somewhere down the road to another pair of underprepared travellers. As for me and Eddie, when we got back to England, our family sat dumbstruck when we told the story. But my favourite part of it didn't happen for another ten years.

One decade later Eddie visited me in Paris. We were reminiscing about that fateful weekend, Mary, and the City of Light. We hadn't discussed the story for years and something about being in Paris together brought the memories flooding back.

"Wouldn't it be amazing to find Mary again?" Eddie said, shaking his head with a smile and wiping croissant crumbs from his chin.

"That's it! What an idea, let's do it!" I responded.

I was always on the hunt for a good story and we had one in our lap. We decided that we had to make it our mission to find Mary, one decade on, and to thank her for her hospitality, not to mention for giving us both a story we'd retold endlessly over the years. And what better way to document the journey than to record it as a podcast episode?

We didn't have her contact details, however, and we spent four days retracing our steps, looking for clues, and searching all over the internet for the elusive Mary. I emailed every account that seemed to be tied to her, reached out on every social media profile, but to no avail. The French are notoriously private online; many of my own French friends have fake names on Facebook. Maybe Mary had a fake profile too… We enlisted the help of a beginner tarot card reader and almost hired a private detective until he told us his astronomical fees. It was a cracking ride, and eventually, by looking at old blog entries and photos we traced the story from the Champs-Elysées to the Paris suburb of Courbevoie, right up to the exact apartment building we'd spent the night. We even rode all the way out there on the scooter. But there was no Mary in sight. The lobby was open and we scoured the names on the intercom dials; nothing seemed to match.

As a last resort, we stood out on the street and looked to the balcony on the top floor, the balcony that featured in our photographs all those years ago, and we saw an open door. It was our last hope. I asked Eddie to yell out for Mary, to call her name into the Paris skies like a young Australian Romeo. A hail Mary, if you will. And, just like ten years before, he looked into my eyes and said "You know what's best Ol, I'll do it." I fed him the lines.

"MARYYYY!" he called, with me whispering in his ears as he went. He continued to yell.

"We're the two people you looked after ten years ago! Here, seeking salvation."

I admit, I got carried away with the last bit, but it was clear that Mary wasn't there. She'd probably long since moved away. We were on a wild goose chase. And while it made for a fun podcast episode, the hunt for Mary ended in failure. Eddie was despondent, but I told him that Mary would have been happy anyway. In our search for her we'd scooted across the whole city, and in a roundabout way had experienced the true Paris. We'd met the locals, passed countless tourist hotspots, and even dared to cross the Paris ring road to get a taste of suburban life. I released the episode about our journey, and judging by the response, I disappointed a lot of listeners by the fact that we never found Mary. It was disappointing for me too, I'd always hoped to be reconnected with her.

Many months later, I got an unexpected email from a woman called Mary. *The* Mary. *Our* Mary. She'd checked her old email account, seen my messages, followed the links and she had found our podcast episode. She'd listened with her whole family, the same family who'd taken us in a decade earlier. As I read her message I was terrified that she would be unhappy or uncomfortable with being the subject of an episode, but it was rather the opposite.

"Oh, it was wonderful!" she wrote, adding how pleased she was to get her 15 minutes of fame, or as she called it, her *fameux quart d'heure de gloire*, which I much prefer.

"We sometimes talk about you two, too," she added. "You can't imagine what a delight you were to have around. I'm so happy you came by the tourism office that day and didn't sleep in the wild."

She added that she had left Paris for a quieter life in the south of France. A life where she didn't feel like she had to take pity on orphaned tourists, no doubt. I've never made it to her corner of France and she hasn't been back to Paris, but I hope one day to meet Mary once more and to thank her for one of my most memorable nights in Paris.

6.5 The cheese

It was a warm April night in Paris and I was sitting in a pool of what may have been someone else's sweat. I'd just finished another basketball game in the secret Marais league and was hanging out courtside with two guys from Normandy.

"So are you guys gonna play next week?" I asked.

"Ah, next week is a *mois de Gruyère*, there won't be much basketball," responded Mathieu, a gentle giant of a Frenchman.

I gave him a blank look.

"A *mois de Gruyère*?" I asked.

"Yes, a Gruyère month," he said with a chuckle. "There are so many public holidays in May that it's like a Gruyère cheese - full of holes!"

Ah. I apologized that my knowledge of French cheese still wasn't at the level where I used it to describe calendar months.

"*Mais non*, Oliver," he said. "Gruyère isn't a French cheese. It's Swiss. Don't tell me you don't know your French cheeses?"

Arnaud, the other basketballer, leaned in, eyeing me up with suspicion. No point lying, I figured, and admitted that I was more or less clueless.

"So what do you buy when you go to the *fromageur*?" asked Arnaud, the slightly-less-towering Norman.

I told the truth. Ever since my humiliating failure at the fromagerie when I first moved to Paris, I'd been too scared to venture inside another cheese shop again. If I wanted cheese, I got it from the supermarket.

It was almost as if I'd offended them personally. They threw their hands in the air and scoffed loudly.

"Think of what you've been missing out on! For two years! This won't do, you can't live in France without knowing French cheese. Soon you'll tell us you don't know French wine."

I let my silence do the talking. And it wasn't long before it was decided. The mammoth Norman basketballers would be my culinary gurus. If you're going to live in France, they said, you need to have a good grasp of the cheese and wine. And they were going to teach me.

On Tuesday the next week, there was a knock on my front door and the Normans lumbered in, arms laden with heavy bags. I was ready with a few glasses of cider from Normandy, which they took with great pleasure. In an attempt to make them feel at home, I pointed out that I'd even brought back a bottle of Calvados, an apple brandy, after a recent trip to their region. They beamed with pride.

They cleared our kitchen table, a small square-shaped island in the middle of the room, and took to laying out various cheeses and bottles of wine with great care. All the while they were particular about me and Lina staying out of the way and leaving them to it. They argued between themselves in angry whispers, apparently about where some of the cheeses should go on the table. Eventually, they invited Lina and I to join them. What they'd done was incredible. The table was covered with cheeses of every shape, size, and colour imaginable. But I still couldn't figure out why they'd been so careful with the placements. It seemed haphazard, unusual.

"*Alors, mes amis,* welcome to the cheese and wine map of France," said Mathieu with a grin. "This table is France, yes? We're here, in Paris," he said, pointing vaguely to the top middle section of the table.

"This is north, this is south, yes?" Arnaud chimed in.

"Right. Now, listen carefully, we're about to teach you all you need to know about cheese, and we're going to explain your dinner."

With great pride, the two Normans picked up each piece of cheese, told us its name, explained the region it was from, made us smell it, then placed it back on the table. They took special pride as they showed the Camembert, which is perhaps the most famous cheese from their beloved Normandy region.

Then they did the same thing with the wine, with some familiar names, like Bordeaux and Burgundy, set clearly in their geographical homes on the table, alongside other red wines with names I'd not heard before.

"Now, let's get started."

We then proceeded to eat the entire table full of cheese. They taught us how to slice it, the stories behind the cheeses, and for what occasions we should buy them. It was fascinating. Some of the cheeses I'd heard about before, but most were new to me and wildly exotic. There was a Tomme de Savoie, a mild Alpine cheese that became an instant favourite. There was a Timanoix from Brittany, a cow's milk cheese made by monks. There was a Crottin de Chavignol, a tasty goat cheese from the Loire Valley, and a semi-hard blue cheese from Auvergne called Fourme d'Ambert. The most visually impressive was the Coeur Neufchatel, which was shaped like a heart and is said to be one of the oldest cheeses in France. There was also a particularly stinky Munster Ferme from Alsace, so soft that it was almost a liquid. The basketballers took great care to explain exactly how to order the cheese too - there's nothing to be scared of, they said. Don't hesitate to tell the *fromageur* if you only want a little, and don't be afraid to ask questions, because it will often lead to a free tasting sample.

Now, this lesson, as you may imagine, wasn't rushed. My friends went into great detail; they truly wanted me to understand and appreciate this integral part of life in France. And as the hours passed, we also managed to drink all the wine. Let me tell you, those Normans could drink. And as a grateful host, I did my best to keep up with these monstrous Obelixes, and I'd done pretty well, if I'm honest. But I must admit, as my bedtime approached I was glad when the last bottle was emptied. I couldn't have managed another drop. All on a Tuesday too.

It was around this point that Mathieu's eyes started scanning the room.

"Now, what were you telling us about that bottle of Calvados?"

Merde.

6.6 Faking French

When I was a boy, my mum convinced me and my brothers that she could speak French. With the fluency of a Parisienne she would burst into a dramatic flurry of what sounded to us like perfect French. How did she learn it? Why did she learn it? We never thought to ask. We were just impressed by this amazing talent.

It wasn't until many years later that we learned she had been… gasp… *faking* French. I suppose for us children the idea that someone could fake a language by imitating the sounds was a *foreign* concept, for the want of a better word. But she fooled us alright. Looking back, I can still remember the noises she made. A lot of zhe sounds, as in the je in *je m'appelle.* There were also a lot of soft p sounds, like the pom in the word pomp. I suppose it was a lot of *je pom pom, la la la* and so on. She was quite convincing; she even had the shrug and the hand gestures.

I sometimes wonder if it was my mum's impression that got me hooked on French, or at least on fake French. At the very least, I'm certain she got me into my fascination with languages and accents. And believe me, I *am* fascinated by accents. When we drove across America my biggest pleasure was hearing how people's accents seemed to change with every state. I still wish I'd documented it somehow.

Anyway, now I was in Paris and thinking of ways to give the podcast a bigger following. I had no budget, which by now should be such a familiar plot point to you that I hardly need to mention it any-more. Essentially, I was thinking of ways to promote my show for free. I reflected on the viral video I'd done in Sweden, the one about the sharp intake of breath to say "yes". If millions of people would watch a video about *that* language oddity, then surely I could recreate something sim-ilar in France. But in Sweden, I'd had the luxury of a camera operator, an editorial team, and a video editor. Now I only had myself, an iPhone, and a girlfriend. If I was going to do a video, it would have to be with the minimum amount of equipment and technical expertise possible.

While I couldn't think of a language quirk that would match the one in the Swedish video, I suppose I inadvertently took inspiration from my own mum and filmed a short clip about how to fake a French accent. I mulled over the script for a week or two until I had perfected it, then waited for a day with blue skies to film it. And one brisk day while passing the Eiffel Tower on foot, I decided it was go time. Lina held the camera and I spoke for 67 seconds - all in one take (so I wouldn't have to edit it afterwards). This is what I said, more or less word for word.

"OK guys, here's how to imitate a French person in four steps, even if you can't speak French.

Imitate a horse. Purse your lips gently and exhale hard. It helps to lift your shoulders and look confused.

Imitate a monk. You know that humming hymn-like noise? Eurgh.. Do that whenever you're lost for a word or need to fill a gap.

Learn a few Paris Metro station names and say them regularly. *Barbès Rochechouart, Jaurès,* and *Sentier* are some particularly good ones to start with.

Most importantly, learn the French swear word *putain* (and say it often).

Then you just mix all four of these together and you're faking French. It should sound something like this:

Ah oui eurgh putain... Barbès Rochechouart eurgh... Sentier putain eurrrgh."

That was it. Now, while that last sentence might not look particularly French to you, if you say it out loud with just enough of a lilt to your voice then I can guarantee anyone near you will say "By God I didn't know you spoke French". Try it!

OK maybe not, but one thing I do know is that there was a truth to my observations, because when I uploaded the clip to Facebook all hell broke loose. The views instantly started to rack up. You know you're onto something when the first thousand come quickly. Remember, at this time I didn't have a strong following online; the show was still quite new. But people were finding this video and they were sharing it. While the views kept racking up, the shares were flying at an unheard of rate, for me at least. 5,000, 10,000, 50,000 shares. If you consider that was just the number of people *sharing* it, imagine how high the view count was! It was unbelievable. It had worked! Sixty-seven seconds of me faking a French accent was getting passed around online quicker than I could keep up with it. I started getting messages from friends in Paris and around the world who'd found the video. French people were extremely vocal with their thoughts on the imitation, and most seemed to find it pretty spot on.

By the end of the day I had to turn off all notifications from Facebook because it was getting shared so much. Before that day, I'd taken great pleasure to read every comment that anyone had ever left. Heck, I even responded to them all. And I did it on this video too, but only for the first ten comments or so. After that it was madness. The view just kept soaring. 100,000, 200,000, 500,000 hits. It was around this point that other pages started downloading it to their computers then reuploading it to their own channels. I started to see it popping up everywhere as people started sharing their pirated versions, some with subtitles for foreign languages. Yes, it burned too fast and it got away from me. I'd predicted this might happen so I added text to the video mentioning The Earful Tower, and I'm glad I did. As my video reached the 1 million view mark on Facebook, I saw that other versions of my video were flying even higher. One of them is up at 4.5 million hits as I write this. But that's fine, it was all just spreading the message. The original version of my video plateaued at around one million hits, which I considered to be astronomical. I can't even guess how many people have seen it in total. Ten million? More? Who knows.

All I really cared about was that the idea had worked. People who liked what they had seen were now following my Facebook page and I've never had a boost like it since. On a budget of zero euros I'd reached millions. When the dust settled, I was left with around 10,000 Facebook followers. To this day I still meet people who recognize me from that video. I've even had a few people quote it to me. An older American guy once crossed the room at an event to speak to me, then said "Barbes Rochechouart eurrrrrghh" before walking off without another word.

As lovely as it was to have a new following, the show was just like the vast majority of other blogs and podcasts out there in that it still brought in nearly no money. In fact, it was actually costing me, considering the hosting fees and the website charges. Still, I figured if I could make millions of people watch something, surely I could make a living out of it.

But how?

CHAPTER SEVEN

A proposal, teaching at
university, and World
Cup pandemonium.

7.1 The podcast

The new podcasting studio was in another *chambre de bonne* - a tiny maid's quarters - on rue Lafayette near the Gare du Nord train station. Of course, there was no elevator, so that meant trudging up six flights of steps, often with a guest in tow. And if I thought my first apartment was petite, this one took first prize. I feel sorry for any maid who lived in it. It was a square room, the length of a pool table, though it did have a nice little view. There was a table in the middle with a few micro-phones facing the chairs, a small desk to one side, and a mini fridge in the corner. And it did the trick perfectly. Imagine, a radio studio in the heart of Paris, broadcasting to the world from under the rooftops.

I did weekly episodes with special guests, and I was getting to meet some interesting faces from the Paris scene. I'd started with bloggers, food writers, YouTubers, and authors, and moved on to comedians, actors, and tour guides. I talked to cafe owners, chefs, priests, photographers, TV stars, ambassadors, and mayors. If someone had something to say about life in France, I was there to listen. As all of these people shared their podcast appearances with their own fans, the show gained new followers; and it was encouraging to see the downloads grow.

I spent so much time in the studio that the radio station eventually gave me my own key. I could use the space whenever I wanted. I taught myself more about the production side of things; how best to edit audio, and surprised myself by enjoying it. Editing audio is like being able to speak a secret language. If you wear headphones and edit in public, like on a plane or in a cafe, then the person next to you can watch your every move and have no idea what you're doing. All they see are the squiggly lines, like a heart monitor.

But what was I actually editing on the shows? The truth is: not much. One of the joys of recording the podcast episodes was that I did it like it was live. If a neighbour started drilling, if an alarm went off in the distance, if someone walked into the studio - and all that has happened - then I just rolled with it and left it in the final recording. This was partly because I liked the flow of a live show and thought it was more authentic. But also because it made for less editing work. And people seemed to like it. I'd get emails from nostalgic travellers who felt they were in Paris again when they heard a siren in the background and thought, even for the briefest of moments, that the siren was outside their own window. I was learning that if I couldn't bring these Francophiles to Paris, at least I could bring Paris to them.

All the while, the emails continued to pour in. One woman said she'd been inspired to move to Paris after listening to the show (and apparently she did!). There were little groups of listeners in pockets around the world who'd meet to discuss recent episodes, guests, and their own dreams of Paris.

It was around this point that I considered getting sponsorships, but I had no idea how to do it. I'd never worked in sales and marketing, I was unorganized, and I didn't know where to start. But, as fortune would have it, an email dropped into my inbox with an opportunity for a new experience and the chance to pay off a few bills.

7.2 The teacher

When you move to a new country, the three-year mark is an achievement that grants you access to an elite club. It's impressive to newer expats and even to French people. It's almost like you can be taken more seriously, because you've served your time, and you've earned some respect. In any case, on the day of my three-year anniversary in France, I got an email from a professor at the American University of Paris.

"Oliver, would you be interested in teaching podcasting to undergrads as a side gig?" he wrote. "Maybe we can go for a coffee and a chat?"

I met the professor soon after on the Left Bank in a little cafe of his choice, not far from the university and in the Eiffel Tower's shadow. He ordered *café crèmes* for both of us and dipped his croissant into the coffee as he spoke. He was obviously a lifer; only the French dunk their pastries in coffee. I dunked mine too, as if it were the most normal thing in the world, and put the disgusting wet pastry into my mouth.

"Why's everyone obsessed with the Right Bank these days? Those fuckers have no idea. What, there's a few new coffee shops? There's nothing over there that the Left Bank can't offer," he said.

I had been about to mention how pleasant it was for me to have ventured across the river for a change. I kept quiet.

"I saw you did a whole episode about the Left Bank," he said. "Good, good. Anyway, I'll cut the bullshit. Podcasting is the new side of journalism, right? So our journalism students need to learn it, yes? And you can teach them, right? If so, come next Thursday."

That was it. We organized the rest over email, and as I scooted to the safety of the Right Bank, I wondered what had happened.

I taught a few different groups of students over the coming months. They were doing degrees in anthropology, journalism, and sociology, and their professors wanted to keep up with the online world. I taught the students how to record audio, edit it, add sound effects, and clip it all together into a short "podcast". The results were usually impressive and it felt good to pass on some of the lessons I'd learned.

But while I enjoyed teaching, nothing could beat the scooter drive to the university. I'll go out on a limb and say it was the best scooter commute in the world. Imagine this: I started in the 11th arrondissement, headed down past the Place de la République and the towering statue of Marianne, the symbol of France. Then I ducked left, passed alongside the colourful Pompidou museum of modern art; then zipped across the Seine River with the Notre Dame cathedral to my left. When I reached the Left Bank, I turned right and followed the Seine almost all the way to the Eiffel Tower, passing the Musée d'Orsay, which was once a train station and now is home to a world-class art collection. I also passed between the gold dome of the Invalides and the extravagant Pont Alexandre III bridge. As the Eiffel Tower got closer, I swung left, parked the bike, and taught the students, while still on a Paris high from that glorious ride. And to think that just a year earlier I'd have taken the Metro.

7.3 Smile!

People warn you that you shouldn't smile in Paris. What nonsense. Don't listen to those miserable people. Listen to me instead. You *should* smile in Paris. You should smile everywhere, too, not just here. Haven't they done studies that smiling in general makes you happier? Why not smile now? Right now? Maybe have a little chuckle so the person near you wonders what you're reading. Go on, really sell the chuckle. They'll probably ask about this story. Show them the cover. Tell them about the book. Heck, maybe even get them to subscribe to the podcast.

Did you do it? Or are you alone in a room? Doesn't matter, smile anyway. There, now you're feeling better, aren't you?

Anyway, the point is that people are ultra friendly in Paris if you walk in with a smile. I'm talking about shopkeepers, cafe owners, waiters, bartenders, bankers - those kinds of people. No need to smile on the Metro or the street, or wherever you don't feel like getting unwanted attention. I've found that starting an interaction with a smile will open all kinds of doors in Paris. I had Caroline de Maigret on my show once, the supermodel who wrote "How to be Parisian Wherever You Are", and she was smiling the whole time. She even smiled in a photo I took with her after the recording. On the show she said: "Smile and talk nicely and people will be nice. You should smile in life. I want to be living in a world where people are actually nice and smile and try to be good to each other. That's the world I want to live in".

So where did this myth come from that Parisians don't smile? Who cares? The point is, you should ignore it. Instead, here's my little tip if you want to make a Parisian smile back at you. Now this only really works if you speak a tiny bit of French (and not too much, mind you).

You go into the shop or cafe, smile at the person, and when they say *bonjour*, you respond with "*Bonjour, ça va?*", meaning, "Hello, how are you?" Any Parisians reading this will scoff, as will most French people in general, because it's absolutely not done in France. French people *never* ask strangers how they're going. What a waste of time! And they don't care either. And to be fair, why *would* you care?

But that's the whole point. I know this is true, and yet I'm doing it still, on purpose. You see, *ça va,* these two little words and four letters, are playing an enormous role in setting the scene and putting you in it.

All in the space of one second, you've made it clear that you're a foreigner. You've also shown that you're a friendly foreigner, a smiling, friendly foreigner. Yes, you're a foreigner who is breaking the code of never asking strangers how they're going, but you're also making an effort to speak French. And no matter how good your French accent is, they'll also glean that you're still learning; because no fluent French speaker would go around saying "*ça va*" to strangers.

Like I said, there's a lot going on here. But I'd wager that four times out of five, they'll roll with you and smile too. Hey, they might even ask you where you're from. Once I said *ça va* and the *monsieur* concluded that I was Canadian, since I was being way too friendly for a Frenchman. They'll often laugh too; at least they do with me, because for some reason it's such an unusual situation in France to ask someone you don't know "How are you?" that it's downright funny. So, if you're feeling plucky and fancy a conversation, this is perhaps the best way to start it. It's a guaranteed smile.

If you enjoyed that tip, I've got one more for you. People in France will affectionately joke that someone who can't speak the local lingo "speaks French like a Spanish cow" (*Comme une vache espagnole*). I've no idea what a Spanish cow has done to deserve this little simile, but I *do* know that it's a great gateway into a conversation. Instead of saying "I don't speak French" or "My French isn't very good", do as I do and say *Je parle française comme une vache australienne* ("I speak French like an Australian cow"). You see what I did there? I switched 'Spanish' to the much more personally relevant 'Australian'. It works wonders. It'll loosen the mood, let them know you're not a fluent French speaker, let them know you have a sense of humour, and even let them know where you're from. Try it! All you need to remember is to change *australienne* to wherever you're from. Perhaps you're a *vache americaine*, or *anglaise*, or *peruvienne*. Wherever you're from, just remember to make the nationality feminine to match the cow (even if you're a man). Although, to be completely fair, if you're saying you speak French like an American cow then it might even sell it better to get the cow's gender mixed up.

The point with all this is that whoever started this story about not smiling in France is some miserable old cow with no sense of humour. Don't be like that person. Be a happy cow and smile about it.

Yes, smile and the French will smile with you.

7.4 The proposal

It was somewhere around this point that I proposed to Lina. Life with
her was too wonderful, so I bought a ring, hid it in my pocket, then
proposed to her on a rainy night in Paris. Right in the middle of the
bridge by the Louvre. You already know this story, remember? It was
at the beginning of the book. It was quite a special night, even besides
the engagement. We'd decided to tie in John Baxter's birthday party
with cocktails at the Ritz, which had been a Christmas present from my
parents. It turned out to be one of the most memorable nights of our
lives. The Ritz bar, where we headed after the proposal, was impressive
too. We didn't bother telling the staff that we'd just gotten engaged,

instead we enjoyed the wildly expensive cocktails with glowing smiles on our faces. Then, as we left, we called our families to share the news, and there were tears of joy from Australia to Sweden.

When I later told Baxter about the proposal, the bridge, the rain, and the Ritz, he said it should be the first chapter of this very book. Good thinking, John! There was no denying it, we were in love. (Me and Lina, of course, not me and Baxter. Baxter and I were just friends.) But as for Lina, well I proposed to her in December and we decided to get married in July, in Sweden. Sure, six months isn't a very long engagement but why wait?

We had initially planned to have a small ceremony in a French chateau after the fun of my 30th birthday party, but the more we looked into the logistics of getting married in France, the more we shied away from it. If I thought the admin for getting a new bank account was difficult, imagine the paperwork for two foreigners to get married. After some deliberation - where *does* an Australian marry a Swede, anyway? - we decided that it would be easiest to tie the knot in Sweden. Lina's parents offered their back garden for the reception, in a small village called Mariefred outside of Stockholm, and that was that. We settled on a date, invited friends from around the world, and we booked a church for the ceremony.

In Sweden, it's customary to meet with the local priest ahead of the wedding so they can get to know you and learn your story. We met ours in the town's white stone church, which was built in 1624 and stands proudly on a little hill by the lake. Our priest, a soft spoken man in his fifties with the faintest hint of a lisp, took us to his office to flesh out the details. When we asked if he could hold the ceremony in half-English, half Swedish, he admitted that he'd struggle with the English part. We said we didn't mind if his speech was a little Swenglish; but I was more concerned that he couldn't pronounce my last name.

My last name, Gee, is pronounced exactly like the seventh letter of the alphabet in English. But he kept saying Oliver *Yee*, explaining that the Swedes simply don't have the soft G sound like English people have, in words like genius or gem. The priest looked at me in consternation. And *I* was worried that Lina would be married to Oliver Yee, and not me.

"I know!" I said. "It's pronounced Gee as in Jesus. Gee-sus!"

The priest looked dismayed.

"But in Sweden we call Him *Yeesus*," he responded with a sigh.

It crossed my mind to suggest he say *Chee*, which sounds more like Gee than Yee does, but I feared he would end the ceremony with "I now present the Cheese".

The priest promised he'd practice his pronunciation - and I went back to Paris to knuckle down on work. After all, I thought, who wants to marry a struggling podcaster?

7.5 The salary

Even though podcasts have been around for decades, believe it or not, there's no script for how to make money out of them. Adverts are the obvious answer, but I didn't know how to get them, and was reluctant to dilute the show with promotions about mattresses, as many other shows do. At this point, I'd been running the podcast for about a year, and I was still broke. Sure, I'd given the occasional walking tour, put on a couple of live shows, and taught podcasting classes at university, but I had no regular income by any stretch of the imagination. So I was left with one probing question: How *do* you make money out of a podcast? This is, incidentally, the question that I get asked the most in my life, so here's the answer, once and for all, and how I figured it out.

While I didn't have a salary, I did have a following. And it was a kind and generous set of followers. I'd met with many of them over the previous year; they often told me that they were coming to Paris and would love to buy me a drink. In those days I met with everyone, thrilled to know that *anyone* was listening to my show. I used to be so flattered that I would even buy the listeners drinks as a thanks. It was surreal to meet actual human beings who listened to the show, because up to this point they'd been just emailers or online statistics.

After a while, as I met more listeners, I stopped buying the drinks - that wasn't helping with the whole salary thing. But I still met them, and I started to see a pattern. Firstly, it was clear to me that many of them were Paris addicts, desperate to soak up anything about this enchanting city. And I'd been quenching their thirst for Paris while joining them on their often long commutes on the other side of the world. And unlike the other Paris blogs, books, or YouTube channels, I was quite intimately introducing the listeners to real-life characters who made the City of Light shine. Giving the guests 30 minutes to talk about themselves and Paris revealed a raw and honest perspective on the city that people weren't getting elsewhere.

But the funny thing was that many of the listeners felt like they knew me too. I mean, I suppose I *was* sharing a fair chunk of my own life, but it was fun to see how listeners handled this differently. Some figured that since they knew me, I must know them too; so they'd sit down and start telling me about their lives, their hometowns, and what they were doing in Paris. Others would sit silently and wait for me to talk, perhaps feeling like they didn't want to interrupt the live podcast they were experiencing. Some wanted to pick my brain about what to do in Paris, or how they could move here. But heck, everyone was different, and I was happy to meet them all. Some listeners took it a step further, sending me photos of their pets, or gifts in the mail, like books about Paris, or treats from their home city. As time passed, some would invite me to dinners, parties or trips out of Paris. Eventually I decided to draw a line - and I drew it at meeting for a coffee.

But, the problem remained: as pleasant as it was to meet new people and to be treated to a drink, I needed to turn a switch somewhere and somehow create a salary - otherwise I couldn't justify doing the show anymore. The podcast was getting around 30,000 downloads a month, which I learned - in those days at least - was enough to put it in the top 10 percent of all podcasts in the world. Not bad for a one-man job, not least considering how many other podcasts had big companies behind them, or came from radio stations like the BBC.

So rather than trying to get advertising, I decided to try to get the listeners to fund the show. I discovered a crowdfunding website called Patreon, which allowed followers to give regular pledges to small creative platforms. It was like a magazine subscription. People paid a monthly fee, but instead of getting a magazine, they got some kind of extra access. It took me a while to figure out what to give in return for people's subscription, and how much to charge for it. But as luck would have it, my crowdfunding launch occurred at the same time as Facebook rolled out live videos, where you can press "record" on a "live stream" and the followers would get a notification to watch. And it made sense for me. Paris is the most beautiful city on the planet, so why should I only focus on audio? I decided to carry out bonus interviews with my guests as we walked around in Paris, pointing out anything worth seeing. It was kind of like a talk show, but while walking: I called it a "walk show," and that was that.

The podcast remained free, but if you wanted to see the live Walk Shows, you'd have to become a paying member. I made it clear from the outset that membership wasn't a sympathy crowdfunding thing; rather, it was access to a club where people could choose to see more of Paris. It felt like a pretty big risk at the time, because it meant doing a lot of extra work and then "hiding" it. But I took the chance and I did it, and I'm glad I did. The early days were rough. There were so few members and they were spread out across the world. This meant that if I were to do a live video in the morning, the Americans would be asleep and I'd have to hope an Australian or two was awake. The first Walk Show I did was me alone, walking around the Left Bank, and only one viewer tuned in. It seemed so hopeless, so pointless, and I felt like I was wasting that one person's time - yet I pushed on. Because I believed in the idea.

Gradually, more members joined and I made more live videos. I made them as engaging and as interactive as possible. If someone at home typed a question in the comment field, I'd answer it or read it out to the guest as it came in. It was live, and it was raw. I took cues from the audience, zooming in on something they'd seen in the distance, showing the road signs so they could find the same streets for themselves, and making them feel like they were in Paris too. The advantage I had over all the countless travel shows about Paris and beyond was that my shows were immediate and in real time. There was no editing; if something went wrong, we had to deal with it on the spot.

And believe me, things went wrong in those early days. Once I did a video with the Australian ambassador to France, Brendan Berne. It was a huge deal for me, the first guest where I had to go through a press team. They'd put the word "Unclassified" on all their emails, which made me nervous from the outset. We were to walk along the Bir Hakeim bridge by the embassy - the same bridge from the opening scene of *Last Tango in Paris*. I planned to do the same walk as Marlon Brando had done before me. The ambassador's press team followed us along worriedly in the distance; the same press team that had advised him against doing a live video. And they were right to be concerned. When I pressed the "live" button on my phone and we started the show, my camera equipment went berserk. The stabilizer spun out of control like a headless chicken, like something from *The Exorcist*. And there was nothing I could do about it, it was live. I forced the camera into submission and I tried to steer a serious interview while the camera kept trying to spin. The ambassador laughed it off, but I still have nightmares about it. It's a wonder he ever agreed to let me host a blowout soirée in his magnificent residence one year later; but that's for the end of the book.

Those early Walk Shows, they were a crazy ride, I can tell you. If you've never seen one of them, let me explain why they're so mad. First, I had to concentrate on operating the camera to focus on me and the guest (or whatever we were looking at). Second, I needed to make sure we were going the right way, and never just standing still. That's crucial: we had to be walking, otherwise we might as well have stayed in the studio. Plus, Paris was the real guest of the video, and people wanted to see it. Third, and perhaps most importantly, I needed to maintain an engaging conversation with the guest, keeping in mind that they weren't always comfortable with being live on the internet. Fourth, I needed to make sure I was keeping an eye on the comments from people tuning in from around the world, because without them, there was no point doing it live. Interaction was key. And last of all, I needed to make sure I wasn't going to get hit by a car or step in any surprises that a dog or a horse may have left behind.

Yes, it was mad but I absolutely loved it. And I was fortunate that at the time, no one else was doing live interviews on the streets of Paris. It was something new, and there was an appetite for it.

As I started to promote the membership platform more, and as I managed to convince more guests to go for a walk with me, the members began to sign up more regularly. Gradually, the Paris podcast fans became too curious about the videos - or maybe they just wanted me to succeed - but either way, they kept trickling in and the group kept growing. It wasn't a quick process, but I gave it my all. When I hit that "live" button I'd find people were ready and waiting, and there'd be 15 people watching, where once there was only one. I got to know the names of the more talkative members and learned their personalities from their comments. Kerrin in Australia would never miss a show. Brian in Victoria would always be first with feedback. Cindy and James in Chicago would set an alarm and get up at any hour to watch. Deborah in Virginia would always be the first to comment.

This thing was growing. I stopped doing all other forms of work, whether it was freelance journalism or teaching at the university, and I set my sights on a tangible target - reaching France's minimum wage via podcast subscription. If enough members joined the club, if my total monthly earnings could equal that of the elusive minimum wage, then it would be official. It would be a job.

Around nine months after I did the first-ever Walk Show with its solitary home viewer, the collective monthly pledges added up to match the minimum wage. It was an incredibly satisfying feeling. Yes, I'd invented a job. My own job. As a podcaster, no less. Now, I don't know, this might not sound like such a big deal to all you people out there earning much more than minimum wage, but for me it was such a validating moment that I could have cried. Sure, I was only earning the kind of money that I could get flipping burgers at a fast food joint, but I didn't care. I had quit my old job, aimed to make it on my own, and I'd done it.

7.6 The catacombs

There's a certain point in the life of a podcast where things just change. It's definitely not an overnight thing, but there's a perceptible point where you realize it has become its own entity. It could be when it starts to earn money, but I don't think that's really it. I think it's more about the moment when people start to accept its existence. I suppose it's like anything: trends, fashion, computer games. As long as enough people give it a seal of approval, the crowds will follow. For me, I started to realize that it had become a real thing when I started to get much more regular emails.

Sometimes they were really touching; people who said they used the show as a kind of therapy when they were going through hard times. Some people emailed to tell me how they bonded with their loved ones while cooking at home, with my show on in the background. Others said they had binge-listened to all the episodes back-to-back on long road trips. These were my favourite emails, especially when people told me where they were listening. One had his earphones in while mowing the lawn in Texas. One listened while doing the laundry in Peru. There was one fan on the commuter trains of Tokyo, and there was a fairly vocal Fiji contingent. In fact, it was quite easy to organize the statistics to see which cities the downloads were coming from, and it boggled my mind. There were listeners in Greenland, Namibia, and Jamaica. There were listeners on islands I'd never heard of before. And all this added a weird kind of pressure. I felt that even though it was just an independent little show, I had a responsibility to give it my best shot; and so I did.

In addition to the listeners, people who wanted to be guests on the show would email me. This was often exciting too. At first the emails were often way off the mark, but sometimes there were nuggets of gold, like the beekeeper. He'd heard about the podcast through a friend and told me he'd like to show me something special. He explained that he kept beehives on top of the city's prominent buildings and made his own Parisian honey, which was impressive enough. But he wanted to show me his latest project - honey wine. Or mead, I suppose it's called. And where do you think he aged the mead? Down in the catacombs, of course. But not in the touristy part with all the skeletons; no, he had a private little labyrinth that you could only enter if you went through a hospital and gave a secret knock on a door.

I accepted the invite and met him at the hospital. When his colleagues opened the door and let us in, we went down, down, down 30 metres under Paris, into a stone maze. We turned left, right, and left again, all with his pet beagle following along. We eventually came to his corner of the catacombs and we feasted on wine and cheese that was slathered in his own Paris honey. Unfortunately, the beekeeper's English wasn't great, so he never made it onto the podcast, and he was reluctant to let me film in the catacombs for fears that urban explorers would find his secret tunnels (and take his wine). So the beekeeper was never on the show - but his tale remains one of the many follow-up stories I've got in my notes that I hope to share one day. Whenever I think of the beekeeper I wonder just how many stories there are in this city that I've not heard of - and I'm reminded how much I want to find them and tell them.

But these stories were about to take a back seat - I had a wedding to host, a honeymoon to plan, and my Paris mates had organized a bachelor weekend in Amsterdam. And if you think eight mates together in Amsterdam sounds wild, then you'd better strap in. France was about to hold a party that would blow everything else out of the water and into the stratosphere.

7.7 The World Cup

A young woman was standing on the bridge, almost totally naked, and peering down into the murky waters of the Canal Saint-Martin. With one hand she held the railing behind her, plucking up the courage to make the mighty leap into the water below. Thousands stared at her from the waterside, cheering.

"*Allez les bleus!*" she yelled, leaping from the bridge and hitting the water with a splash that was drowned out by the roar of the crowd. As the cheering continued, another man climbed over the railing, and hung from the bridge by his fingertips. With his other hand, he removed his shorts and his bare buttocks shone in the Paris twilight. He hung free and easy in the gentle breeze while the crowd broke into hysterical laughter. Then he let go and fell into the water too. More nudity, more splashes, more cheering. On the road behind them, young men with faces painted red, white, and blue climbed onto moving vehicles, drinks in hand, and danced on the rooftops. All the while, car horns were beeping, people were cheering, and music was playing. And I stood there with mouth agape, wondering what the hell was going on.

Now, of course I actually knew what was happening. France's national soccer team had just beaten Croatia 4-2 and won the World Cup for the first time in 20 years. And it was pandemonium in Paris. But nothing could prepare me for just how extensive the party was. Soccer is like a religion in France, and the celebrations went on long, long, long after the final whistle was blown. I imagine no one got much sleep that night, all on a Sunday too.

For a little perspective, when I first moved to Paris I remember sitting in a pretty typical bar - definitely not a sports bar by any means. On the wall was a digital clock that had stopped ticking. On closer inspection, I saw that it had stopped during the evening of July 12th in 1998. I asked a French friend what had happened at that time and date and he looked at me with a nostalgic twinkle in his eye and said, without missing a beat: "That's when we last won the World Cup. It was the best day of my life".

I am not a huge soccer fan, but I always find mobs of people to be interesting. I walked along the canal trying to fathom why the result of the game had made these people so ecstatic. I filmed a few live videos to capture the mood but the throngs of people all using their phones at the same time meant that the internet didn't last long. I walked towards the Place de la République, the same square where I'd seen millions gather after the Charlie Hebdo attacks. There were similar sized crowds now, but it was a wildly different mood. It was the middle of summer, there was a lot more skin, and a lot more drunkenness.

I wasn't celebrating myself, I was more in a state of hungover confusion. I'd just stepped off the train from Gare du Nord, freshly back from my bachelor weekend in Amsterdam. The trip had been organized by my French mates, the majority of whom had left Amsterdam a day early to watch the final from the safety of home turf. However, I was happy to see the game on the train and to observe the celebrations after. As wild, crazy, and slightly worrying as it all seemed, it felt like the good news that France had been needing for a while. And with my own wedding just around the corner, I was looking forward to some celebrations of my own.

7.8 The wedding

I look back on our wedding in Sweden with mixed feelings. On the one hand it was the best day of my life, joining lovely Lina in holy matrimony and starting our journey of living together happily ever after.

The wedding was wonderful. Friends and family came from afar, our ceremony was in a picturesque Swedish church, the reception was elegant, and the speeches were touching. But on the other hand, an awful lot seemed to go wrong, and I've come to believe that the wedding was ever-so-slightly cursed. And that story's too good not to share, even in a book about Paris.

It was in Paris that the troubles began, in fact. Right as we were heading to the airport to take the last flight of the night we were alerted that our flight had been cancelled. No further explanations were given, no further explanations were needed. It meant that we got to Sweden a day late and via Munich. We arrived to find the country in the midst of a sweltering heatwave. Due to our delay, many of the little tasks we'd left for the last minute were pushed to the last second. For example, just hours before we were to exchange vows, Lina and I were redoing the seating arrangement after an unexpected rethinking of the table layout. No big deal, sure, and we were glad to do it. Even though the heatwave made us wish we were relaxing over a glass of lemonade and sitting by a fan.

The reception was to be held in Lina's parents' back garden, an open-air afternoon and evening. As we fixed the seating plan, we handed the name tags to our family and friends who scurried around, setting them on the tables as directed and putting out cutlery and menus. And oh, what beautiful menus! Lina, who can illustrate even better than she can bake, had designed intricate booklets complete with information about the meals, and also sketches and funny facts about the guests to help them break the ice. Little did we know that almost all of those booklets would be destroyed beyond recognition in just a few hours...

The heat continued to bear down on the little Swedish town as the ceremony drew nearer. Before we knew it, it was time to get ready.

With five minutes until we had to head to the nearby church, one of my brothers said "By the way, does anyone know how to tie a bow tie?"

The answer was no.

None of us had internet connections on our phones and there was no one to help. Everyone else was at the church already, of course. I couldn't help them either (I'd opted for a tie). The boys, none of whom speak Swedish, mind you, ended up running through the town with undone bow ties flailing in their hands, yelling for help. I was striding to keep up with them, cautious of my wedding suit getting ever-stickier in the unbearable heat. As the church bell struck two, the time for our ceremony, I found my brothers in the front garden of neighbours I'd never met before, where some older village locals were helping with the bow ties. Already late, we ran the rest of the way to the church as the sun beat down on us. And when we arrived, the white stone church loomed above us, and I saw a sight that was to be one of the finest of the wedding.

There, in front of the church, were all my friends, who were waiting for us to arrive. Guests had come from five different continents for the big day, and - touchingly - they included our friends from France, many of whom you've met in the pages of this book, and most of whom were so instrumental in shaping my life in Paris. Fabien the Breton was there; so was Stephane, my neighbour. Clovis, my banking aide came along, and so did Cyril, my first-right-then-left kissing mate from Nice. Slim and the Beast, the band that helped me start my show, had brought their guitars from Paris and were to be the evening's entertainment.

Now, you'd typically wait inside the church, of course, but the heatwave had turned the 17th century building into a sauna, and on the hill out the front there was a refreshing breeze. My friends cheered as we all arrived and asked where Lina was, and I admit it was the first time I'd thought about her in hours.

Wasn't she here already? We were already late!

We all rushed up into the church and the priest greeted me, asking when Lina would arrive. I had no idea; she was getting ready in the bridal suite of a nearby hotel. The minutes passed. Soon she was ten minutes late. Then fifteen. The guests inside were sweltering, fanning themselves with Bibles.

But where was Lina? Was she... was she going to leave me at the altar?

I went to the front door of the church again and stood at the top of the steep staircase looking over the town below. Gathered by now was apparently the entire village, no doubt curious about all the foreign guests, the groomsmen running around with their bow ties, and the potential scandal of a missing bride.

She should be here by now. Twenty minutes late? When do I throw it all in and leave?

I looked to the glistening lake by the side of the church, twinkling in the July sunlight. I looked out over the wooden red homes so iconic across the Swedish countryside, and I wondered how an Australian guy like me was getting married in Sweden. Or was *supposed* to be getting married. Then I looked back to the villagers. And what was this? They were poking each other, jostling among themselves, taking our their phones and pointing across the village square. And there, like a beacon of shining light, with two bridesmaids in hot pursuit, came a vision of pure beauty.

My bride.

With a stunning wedding dress she'd made herself, she sailed over the cobblestones of Mariefred with the grace of a movie star. I met her halfway down the stairs. The priest, in a heavy smock and satin sash, breathed a sigh of relief and let the ceremony begin, as the organist played a subtle rendition of "Dancing Queen" by ABBA. We were in Sweden after all.

Lina later told me that because of the extreme heat, she couldn't manage to slip her wedding dress onto her body. The hotel had no air conditioning, and she had spent half an hour wriggling into the dress. In the rush and nervous haste, she had left the hotel at a trot and was sweating almost as profusely as I was. In fact, she almost fainted at the altar as I stood beside her, sweating through my suit. Everyone in the church, including me, was far too busy fanning themselves to notice whether the priest with his strong Swedish accent pronounced my name as Oliver Yee or Gee, and I don't think anyone would have cared either way. The point is, we did it. We were married. We'd gotten hitched without a hitch, or at least without any major ones.

And oh, that moment of leaving the church was miraculous. Everyone could breathe again in the fresh air. Lina's extended family, many of whom were musicians, surprised us all by producing violins, an enormous marching band drum, and huge sprigs of birch trees, and then led us all in procession back to the house to the tune of Swedish folk music. Meanwhile, a French friend, Greg, had brought an unusual music box with him from Paris, which he played at the back of the procession. He'd strapped it to his chest, and when he wound the handle it played songs from his phone - and the faster he wound that dial, the louder the music played. The villagers were loving the show. At the time I thought it was curious indeed that Greg brought such a machine to our wedding, but I'd later thank him for it.

After a morning of madness, everything seemed to have righted itself. Slim and the Beast were waiting at the garden to greet us with an acoustic set as guests mingled over champagne. The sky was bright blue and made a perfect backdrop for family photos. Before long, we sat at the garden tables for the meal. I relaxed, amazed that we'd pulled it off, getting everyone together for a celebration like this. It all seemed too good to be true.

And, of course, it was.

In the space of three seconds, the summer sky turned dark. Clouds hurtled in, draining the colour from the party below. Almost in slow motion, I turned to the father of the bride. He turned to me. We were definitely moving in slow motion. We looked towards the tarpaulins that we had fastened to a nearby wall that morning, ready to be unfurled at the first hint of rain.

But it was too late. A raindrop crashed so hard onto the table between us all that it made a ripple in my wine glass. And then another. A third. In unison, all the guests went quiet and slowly looked up to the heavens.

And then: chaos.

The monsoon that followed was so quick, so heavy, and so violent that no one knew what to do. It was like a dam burst in the clouds and no one could move fast enough. We had 80 people in the garden, most of whom were midway through their first course as the storm struck.

As for us, we'd planned that any rain would be gentle at best and that untying the tarpaulins would be a quick and easy job. But because the rainfall was so furious and fast, and because the covers were folded like a crepe, those folds filled up with water in an instant, making them too heavy to unfurl. Strings that tied them in place snapped. People were screaming. It was like a horror movie.

"Where's Grandma?!" I heard someone yell.

"Take the guitars!"

"Grab the menus!"

Oh God, they had a point. Lina's intricate menus with the sweet little sketches were the first things to be destroyed in the carnage. It's said that only one or two survived. The food was ruined, the wine glasses toppled. Yelling to one another like sailors in a storm, several of the taller guests grabbed anything they could to poke and pull at the tarpaulins, which by now had swollen so much that they were collapsing. Some guests were standing on tables, grasping at the tarps with their hands, only for buckets of rain to waterfall all over them and the tables.

Me, I stood in the middle of it all, wet through and shaking my head in despair. I was speechless. Oh what a disaster, I thought. And what *did* happen to Grandma?

Most of the wedding guests lined up with their backs against the walls, seeking any kind of shelter they could find. My cousin, who was the photographer, couldn't believe his luck and bounded through the chaos snapping away at the whole mess. The rain, like a tropical downpour, continued at full force for five minutes before easing into a gentle shower. But it was too late. It wasn't supposed to happen like this.

The wedding is ruined, I thought to myself.

That is, until something truly magical happened.

From somewhere behind me came the sound of music above the chatter of the guests and the easing rainfall. It was Spanish music, dance music, gently building up and getting louder. I looked around, trying to locate it. The guitars and the speakers had been whisked away, so the music wasn't coming from the band, that much was for sure. But where was it coming from? I spun around, searching for the sound through the rain, the flying tarpaulins, and the soaking guests.

Then I saw him.

It was Greg, the Frenchman, with his music box strapped defiantly to his chest. His white shirt was plastered to his skin from the rain, but he had a determined grin on his face and fire in his eyes. He was winding the handle faster and faster, and the music came out louder and clearer. The music, that sweet music, was drowning out everything else.

Lina's uncle, famed for his speed in hitting any dancefloor, ripped off his tie and fastened it around his head, then stepped out from the shelter and into the rain. At first it was one man, alone, dancing like a maniac as the music box continued to sound its energetic siren call. Then another guest joined the dancing, then another. The music was contagious. Aurelien, the guitarist, found the marching band drum tucked behind a door, strapped it to his own chest, and started pounding it in time to the music. And then quickly, unexpectedly, and miraculously, and as the rain continued to fall on them all, everyone started dancing.

The wedding was saved.

As if we'd been hypnotized we danced until the rain stopped. Even the shyer guests, who'd taken the back seats during the afternoon's proceedings, lost their inhibitions and joined the fun. Meanwhile, the most responsible and practical guests worked furiously in the background, cleaning the tables, sweeping away the water, and removing the soggy menus. Before we knew it, the rain had stopped, the sun was back (this time for good), and we all sat down to enjoy the evening.

I'd love to say the rest of the night was perfect - and it really was close to perfect. In fact, the guests still talk about how the downpour was one of their finest wedding memories. But there was one last cursed surprise for me and Lina.

When we'd danced our last dance and decided it was time to go back to the bridal suite at 4 am, we realized that we'd forgotten one important thing.

"Do you have the key?" I asked her.

Shit. She'd left it in the hotel room in the mad rush to get to the church. And the hotel reception desk was closed for the night. So was the front door to the hotel, actually. And there was no way in. We tried every trick in the book to get into that hotel, but were doomed to fail. We ended up watching the sunrise from the outdoor lounge chairs in the bar. Yes, the bridal suite went unused that night, and we ended up crashing on a mattress in a room of passed-out wedding guests. I fell asleep wondering how it would have gone down if we had rented a chateau in France.

When all the guests had left Sweden, it was time for us to board our own flight back home to France where we'd prepared for a honeymoon adventure. On the plane home, I met an elderly French couple in the seats beside me. They were curious to hear about the wedding, and I mentioned the monsoonal rain. The woman, with a kindly smile, pointed out a neat little bit of French wordplay.

"We have a saying in France: *Mariage plus vieux, mariage heureux*, which means 'An old marriage is a happy marriage,'" she explained. "But another interpretation is: *Mariage pluvieux, mariage heureux*. It's pronounced the same, but it means: 'A rainy wedding makes a happy marriage.'"

The elderly woman smiled at me.

"It rained at our wedding too," she said. "And we've been happy for 47 years."

CHAPTER EIGHT

A mammoth honeymoon
around France.

8.1 The honeymoon

For our honeymoon, we spent two months driving around France
on the little red scooter. We went from Paris to Paris in a huge loop,
travelling 4,000 kilometres at a top speed of 45 kilometres an hour
(that's about 2,500 miles at 30 miles per hour). It was one of the most
challenging and rewarding things I've ever done. But it wasn't easy.
The only easy bit was the planning.

You see, I think travelling is more exciting when you don't know
where you're going - and luckily for me, Lina agreed. We decided to go
big in the plans and not let logic or reality get in the way. Long before
the wedding, we had bought a map of France, pinned it on the wall,
and circled all the places we'd heard about that we wanted to visit.

That was the easiest part, and the towns and cities racked up quickly. Bordeaux and Marseille, obviously. Brittany without a doubt. The Alps and Annecy would be amazing, so would Provence and the Riviera. We'd heard great things about La Rochelle and the nearby island of Ile de Ré - and I was pretty curious about the English-ified villages in the southwest. Not to mentioned Carcassonne and its medieval history, or the famed boardwalks of Deauville to the north.

We stood back and realized that we'd left circles and underlines all over the map and that it would be nearly impossible to see them all. Due to the unusual hexagonal shape of France - the French even call their country *l'Hexagone* - it is a difficult country to explore geographically for a road trip. There's such diversity, and it's so well spread out that you'd be hard-pressed to find the ultimate route. You can't just cross from one side to the other, that's no real achievement. Following the border would mean a mighty 2,913 kilometres (1,810 miles), but then you'd miss a lot of highlights. Sure, you could always zigzag through the country, but then how can you possibly decide where to zig and where to zag? Especially if you start from Paris, which is inconveniently located rather far from the edges.

When we looked hard enough at the map I saw what was obvious. If we started in Paris and headed northwest towards Brittany, then south towards Marseille, then back towards Paris along the eastern side of France, then the route clearly, undeniably, absolutely would make the shape of a heart. Like a frenzied painter working on his masterpiece, I connected the dots and showed Lina the heart shape and watched her raise one eyebrow.

"It doesn't really look like a heart," she said, squinting at the map on the wall. "Maybe an anatomical heart, but not a love heart".

I redrew the lines to make it even clearer. A tighter pinch at Marseille, a wider loop into Brittany - and a similarly wide loop on the way home. If you stood back far enough and squinted hard, the dots undeniably formed the shape of a love heart. Lina burst out laughing but agreed to the idea. Although it was a gimmick, the heart gave us a goal, a plan to stick to and it actually made it much easier to decide where we'd go.

We estimated that we'd spend between six weeks and three months on the road, letting the onset of winter and colder weather dictate the end of the trip. The scooter, after all, was much better suited to riding in the summer sun. The very idea of an adventure with no real end point was so freeing and exciting. Even more so considering we wouldn't have a home to come back to, as our landlady in the 11th arrondissement had decided that she would sell her apartment. The timing was awful, on the one hand, but instead of complaining about it, we decided to see it as a positive sign. An even broader horizon had just opened up and it seemed like the perfect adventure to launch us into married life.

In the excitement of the trip, I mentioned our heart-shaped travel plans in a podcast episode. The next day a game-changing email dropped into my inbox from a listener in Brisbane, Australia.

"Hey Oliver. I've been listening to your podcasts over the last couple of seasons. Congratulations on your engagement! The idea of your round-France journey sounds fantastic, although it sounds more like a slow amble on your 50km/hr max scooter. It will be great to highlight some of La France Profonde. We have a little house in a small village in the Charente. It's a lovely area and you may even be passing through on your journey south. If you're nearby, and are so inclined, feel free to visit the village of Verteuil-sur-Charente for a couple of days and stay at our place *gratuit*, a little wedding gift from one Aussie to another. Cheers and all the best, Jim."

I was speechless. I knew that the podcast had a lot of listeners at this point and I knew that people enjoyed the show, but no one had been so openly generous before. There had to be a catch… what did Jim want in return? Or was his place a wreck? Or was he, could he be… an axe murderer? With the email was a link to his home and it turned out to be one of the most charming I've seen. Nestled in the centre of the medieval village of Verteuil, on the banks of the Charente River, the 18th century stone house was cosy and inviting. Real village life, exactly how I'd imagined the French countryside to be.

I emailed Jim to see if he was indeed an axe murderer, and it turned out he was a kind soul who just wanted to give something back. On the next episode of the podcast I read out Jim's email to thank him, but also to share the developments of the story - and it sparked something I'd never have predicted.

When I woke the next morning, my inbox was flooded with similar emails. Someone with a house in Chantilly; another in Cognac, Nancy, Carcassonne. By the end of the week I had made a folder to keep up with all the offers - together with a map so I could locate these exotic-sounding places. Carpentras, Essoyes, Grenoble, Paimpol, places I'd never even heard about before. Other listeners wrote in and said we could use their frequent traveller points to book hotel rooms. It was unbelievable.

Of all the offers, the one that made the planning the easiest was from Chantilly. Susan, the Irish owner of the property, said her place was available for one weekend in August. Located an hour out of Paris, it seemed like the perfect destination for the first night of the trip. We chose Giverny for the second night, and decided we'd never plan further ahead than that. And it was fortunate that the listeners were so generous, because I was still on minimum wage and we'd be relying on their membership fees to fund our travel. Luckily the scooter only cost five euros to fill up. *Here's to a healthy, carefree, wondrous adventure!* Or so I thought.

8.2 The disease

On an unusually cold and overcast day in mid-August, we packed our luggage onto the back of the little red scooter and headed north out of Paris. It was a 45 kilometre trip to Chantilly, where we'd spend the first night of our honeymoon. As we drove out of Paris and through the suburbs we learned a lot about our limitations almost immediately. The first being that it was pretty hard to figure out which roads we were allowed to drive on. We knew that we couldn't legally take the autoroutes - the kind of highways where cars could get to Chantilly in mere minutes. We had to take the back roads. But we didn't know how to *find* the back roads. At first we experimented with setting the GPS for a bicycle, which worked well. That is, until it would inevitably lead us to a children's park or a little alleyway - neither of which the scooter could cross. A few times on that first day we ended up on big highways where the speed was up to 100 km an hour, and it scared us both. Remember, our scooter could only go 45 km an hour and having trucks whoosh past us was horrifying. Every time we ended up on a major road we took the first available turnoff and headed to the safety of the back streets.

The drive took several hours and left me feeling surprisingly tired. Suspiciously tired, even, but I didn't think too much of it. Susan, our lovely hostess, had organized a cottage for us in the charming town. She walked us over to the Chantilly chateau, which had its own taste of fame as a James Bond movie setting. We even got exclusive access to the royal stables for a video, but all the while I had a niggling feeling in the back of my mind: *Why am I so tired?*

We only stayed one night and moved on towards Giverny, a drive that was more than twice as long as that from the previous day. And as the morning progressed, I couldn't shake the concern about my fatigue. It was worrying me at this point, not least because I started to feel deeply sore over my whole body. I ached, all the way from my shoulders to my legs. I knew riding the scooter would be a challenge, but I hadn't imagined that it would leave me feeling like this. I searched online and found it was fairly normal for motorbike riders to get sore arms and shoulders after long drives, so I tried to ignore it. Surely, after a few days, I wouldn't notice anymore.

But it got worse.

After a few more days I needed to rest after every half an hour of driving. We'd pull over and I'd lay down on the side of the road to recover. In the nights I had cold sweats beyond any I'd experienced before and I was starting to wonder if it was a good idea to continue with the trip. Lina, who at first had said she was also sore from the ride, realized that we weren't on the same playing field and began to keep a close eye on me. It was around this time that an unusual mark appeared on my right thigh, a red rash that continued to grow and sprouted concentric circles.

By the time we reached Deauville on the north coast, a pharmacist said it looked like an insect bite and gave me some cream and headache tablets. I figured that was that. I frolicked on the beach, delighted to walk in the footsteps of Coco Chanel and all the other wealthy Parisians who had flocked to the town for their summer getaways. We were five days into the trip and I was glad my mystery illness would be cured. Despite still feeling pretty grim, I pushed on along the coast to the sobering D-Day beaches, then we marvelled at the medieval tapestry in Bayeux.

But I didn't get any better. One afternoon, a week into the trip, I went to a drop-in doctor in the middle-of-nowhere, Normandy. After three years in France I'd still never been to a doctor, so part of me was quite excited by this new experience. Not least because I was eager to use my social security card that had been so hard to get. My doctor didn't speak English, but there was no mistaking her diagnosis.

"*Oui, ça c'est la maladie de lyme,*" she said after a brief look at the bullseye on my leg.

If you're wondering what that sentence means, then you know exactly how I felt when I heard her say it. What the heck was *maladie de lyme*? Using a little help from the internet, we understood that I'd been bitten by a tick, and that tick apparently wanted to kill me. Perhaps it was a revenge for my fruit fly massacre the previous summer. While

I may not have noticed the tick bite at the time - it had left me with an unusual illness known as Lyme Disease. The main symptoms, the doctor said, included intense fatigue (which can last up to six months), fever, headaches, and joint pain. Well, that sure explained why I'd been feeling so rough. We also learned that if untreated, Lyme Disease can lead to infections of the brain and heart, memory loss, and severe joint problems. Extreme cases can be even worse.

The doctor put me on Amoxycillin and told me to get some rest. We drove less each day, took it easy on the exploring front, and avoided potentially tick-infested areas for safe measure. And it seemed as if the drugs were doing the trick. Indeed, I enjoyed another lovely week of the honeymoon, while my symptoms seemed to disappear.

We explored the northern coastline of Brittany and fell in love with it once again. We revisited Fabien for a lesson in making the local specialty of galette pancakes. We wandered the sands at the mythical abbey island of Mont Saint-Michel, getting lost in its medieval streets. The nearby town of Saint Malo triggered my interest in fortified towns, an interest that would almost overwhelm me by the time we got to Carcassonne. We even got up to Ploumanac'h, a town with remarkable pink granite beaches (not to mention the remarkable apostrophe in its name). We were now two weeks into the honeymoon and decided if we were going to go around the whole country, it was time to escape the northwest and to head south for the first time. We wanted to chase the sun and to find the lavender, the vineyards, and the open road.

Yes, life was good again. It was the honeymoon we were hoping for. We rode in T-shirts and shorts, with the summer sun beating down on us as we headed for the west coast. We were in love, newly married, and were on the open road. And we didn't have a care in the world.

It was around this point, while driving down a road in rural Brittany, that the sun was so strong that it made the back of my neck tingle. Funny how the sun can make you itch, I remember thinking. Lina interrupted my thoughts to say that she had noticed a strange rash on my neck that wasn't there just minutes before. I looked down and saw that the rash had spread to my arms too.

This Lyme Disease wasn't finished with me, it seemed.

8.3 The wolf

They say there are no wild wolves in Brittany, but they're wrong. I saw one. It tried to bite our scooter as we arrived in the village of Guermeur. We'd found a cottage in the woods where I could relax and recuperate for a few days from the Lyme Disease. I was loaded up on antibiotics from the village doctor in Normandy, eleven boxes of pills in total, but this rash was worrying me. By now my chest, back, and legs were covered in spots, and we headed - once again - for a local pharmacy.

We scooted some 10 kilometres out of Guermeur and into La Sourn, population 2,000. The pharmacist took one look at me and said I had to go immediately to a doctor. She was looking worriedly at my throat. My throat? I looked in the mirror to see the rash was spreading quickly, now covering my entire body - even my palms. The local GP was just down the road, and the receptionist told me a doctor was available. Unbelievable, not even a second's wait. Imagine that in Paris!

The doctor, a young man from the area, asked me many questions while inspecting my body. His interrogation gradually drifted further off topic until I realised he was perhaps more interested in something beside my illness.

"And how is your throat?" (Bad.)

"And does this hurt if I press this?" (No.)

"And are you sweating at night?" (Yes.)

"A lot?" (Yes.)

"And how long have you been travelling for?" (Two weeks.)

"And how long will you continue?" (Maybe two months.)

"And where will you go next?" (Vannes.)

I began to realise that these geography questions weren't about nearby doctors or tick-infested national parks. No, he was after something else.

"What about after Vannes?"

"Do you plan to stay in villages or in cities?"

"Have you heard of the Gulf of Morbihan?"

The questions glided smoothly from health to holiday. By the end of the visit I had tips for the entire western coast of France. Almost as an afterthought, the doc told me I'd had an allergic reaction to Amoxicillin, hence the rash. We headed onwards to the chemist at Pontivy to get my new drugs.

"Try and avoid the sun," the pharmacist said, handing me my new pills, Doxycycline. "*Any* exposure to sunlight will cause severe sunburn."

When I told her we were driving a scooter around the country all day and every day, she handed me the strongest sun cream she had and told me to use it liberally and wished us luck. We visited the tourist office in the town, which is inside a *péniche* moored to the canal-side. The woman at the desk said it was the only tourist office in France on a boat. She directed us to the main sites of the town, including a 15th century chateau built in the style of King Philippe Auguste, who was behind the city walls of Paris that had grown so dear to me. Now armed with a good grounding in Pontivy, we dined on *croque monsieurs*, completed the suggested walking tour, then headed back to Guermeur, where the wolf was waiting for us.

I say wolf, and it definitely looked like a wolf, but I suppose it was a Breton Husky on steroids. Whatever it was, it was waiting by a farmer near the entrance to the village, and as we pulled in and drove by it gave chase. The farmer screamed at the hound, something that sounded like "Didier!!!" Now, Didier is a pretty pathetic-sounding name for a wolf-hound, but I wasn't thinking about that at the time. I was focused on two things: the beast tearing after us and the road ahead.

The dog was snarling as got closer. I accelerated as we passed an abandoned church. Lina was yelling as we flew through the cornfields. But I couldn't go too fast, the roads were too small. The wolf gained on us, gained on us, then drew level. He looked at me, my bare left leg, now spotty from the spreading rash, no doubt a tempting treat for a hungry predator. I skidded around yet another corner, where just 24 hours earlier we'd picked blackberries and eaten them on the go. The dog pulled back and started biting near Lina's ankles.

From pure instinct I navigated through the country roads. I tried to put some distance between us and the monster, which I could now see had switched to the right side of our scooter, eyeing up my other leg this time. In the side mirror I saw into its bloodshot eyes, which were looking into mine.

I'm not ashamed to say I was scared. What if the wolf leapt at us? What would I do? The farmer and his screams were now far behind us on the other side of Guermeur. It was just us and Didier. I heard what sounded like the wolf biting the back of the scooter - and it may well have been that - or it may have been a rock hitting the bike, or a screw flying loose as we tackled the uneven terrain.

And just as it was all getting too much, just as I was thinking I'd spend my last moments in the jaws of a Breton wolf, the creature stopped dead in its tracks and turned away, trotting back to his owner. Miraculously, I'd steered us back to our own cottage, which was on a road called "Dead-end swamp" (Impasse des Marais).

We pulled into the driveway and didn't hang around to inspect the bike for tooth marks or blood. Instead, we went inside, shut the door, locked it for good measure, and caught our breath. Then we relaxed. Just as the doctor had ordered. That night, we skipped the sunset walk through the cornfields and stayed inside, watching the sky from the window of our little cottage.

And fancy that - shining stronger than the stars was a perfectly formed full moon.

8.4 The croc

There's no better way to truly experience a country than to see it from a scooter. I've read similar things about riding a motorbike, but we told ourselves that a top speed of 45 km/hour (30 miles) was more pleasurable. Now several weeks into the trip, we were getting used to the slower-paced lifestyle out of Paris and were delighted by the friendliness of the locals.

Elderly ladies would wave at us from their kitchen windows as we chugged by. One time a whole team of village firefighters whooped and cheered as we passed. Every time we stopped for a meal or a snack, shop owners would ask us where we were from, and the further we travelled the more impressed they were with our adventure. One cafe owner stopped us mid- conversation to call over his wife.

"Françoise, come here, this is *énorme*," he yelled, then retold our story using elegant French words and phrases that I noted and tucked away to remember.

It was through these exchanges that I learned how to say words like *périple* instead of *voyage*, which I think sounds much more impressive. I worked on my routine of explaining the trip so well that I knew how to get laughs from the locals. After revealing our top speed, 45 km an hour, I found that if I added "but it's 50 when we go downhill" then even the toughest mechanic would chuckle. The trip was a valuable way to improve our French, as we found ourselves talking about things that never cropped up in daily Paris conversations. We would have to discuss extremely specific directions; or would have to negotiate the price of scooter repairs; or we'd have to eventually master describing the heart-shaped route (*en forme d'un coeur*). Travelling through the countryside of France is an excellent way to improve your French (the scooter bit is optional).

As we continued the trip we were meeting some memorable characters too, perhaps none more so than Éléonore. You may remember the story of the crocodile in the Canal Saint-Martin. Heck, you may even believe it. But a big part of the story that really gave it some credibility was that in 1984, sewer workers found a baby croc near the Pont Neuf on the Seine River. After a short stint in a Parisian aquarium, the reptile was sent to a zoo in Vannes, a town in western France. One of my favourite parts of the story was when I found out that she was still alive all these decades later. But nothing gave me greater pleasure than meeting Éléonore the croc when we passed through Vannes on the road trip. The staff took us behind the scenes to get up close to her. Éléonore, they estimated, was a 40-year-old Nile Crocodile. She was three metres long and weighed 200 kg (10ft and 550 pounds). Part of me was sad to think she'd never taste the local fish of the Nile River. Part of me was sadder still that her enclosure was designed to look like the Paris sewers, where she was found, and not the wilds of eastern Africa. But mostly, I wondered what would become of the two crocodiles in the Canal Saint-Martin in Paris. Would they ever make it to the age of 40?

These were the thoughts in my mind as we continued to head south through the French countryside. As we left Brittany the weather turned even warmer, and we spent long days scooting through the sunflower fields of western France. It was a scorching summer, which I would have loved if it weren't for the damned medication. I was supposed to be avoiding the sun at all costs. Where I'd previously been wearing a T-shirt and shorts, I now had a bandana around my face, sunglasses, a jacket, and gloves. But the sun still found me. By the time we got to La Rochelle my nose and lips had more or less peeled off. As we crossed the enormous bridge to the beautiful island of Ile de Ré, I must have looked like a zombie. But it didn't matter to me; we had finally made it to this popular summer getaway and I was keen to see what the fuss was about.

We stayed in the port town of Saint-Martin-de-Ré, where I'd go through the final hurdle of the Lyme Disease. We rented a tandem bike and set off to explore the salt fields. These fields, or pools really, are laid out like patchwork across the island and are crisscrossed by cycle paths. Locals are on hand, harvesting the salt, and selling it off with salted caramel at mobile stalls. Our tandem ride, which led to a little fishing village, had all the markings of a romantic honeymoon activity. But me, I found it hard to enjoy the romantic part of it all. I was on the front of the bike and the sea salt was so thick in the air that you could taste it. Well, I couldn't taste it - I could feel it. My lips were so badly peeling that it felt like someone was rubbing that salt on my open wounds. Lina was squealing in delight on the back of the bike and I squealed along with her. But little did she know that I was squealing in pain as the thick salty air crucified my raw face. Back near our hotel, I popped into yet another pharmacy for some cream and wondered how many we'd visited so far.

As we watched the sun set over the harbour from our hotel room, I reflected on the honeymoon so far. Sure, there had been a lot of struggles, and it was easy to focus on them. But there'd also been moments of pure romantic bliss. Earlier that day, on the salt field ride, we'd stopped to take in the view. An older man, a local from the village, offered to take our photo as we posed with the tandem on the harbour's edge.

"Don't fall," he said to me. "But then, you've clearly fallen once already. Into the arms of *madame*."

8.5 The breakdown

I heard the helicopter before I saw it. *Thwack thwack thwack thwack,* the blades pounding away dangerously close to the scooter. I scoured the sky above the sunflower fields, but saw nothing. The noise continued as I slowed down, making it immediately and painfully obvious that the thwacking noise wasn't a helicopter at all. It was the front wheel of the scooter. We were in trouble.

I pulled over to a nearby dirt road and parked across the middle of it to investigate. We were in the deep countryside of western France, and far from phone or internet reception. I laid on my back and inspected the damage. There were two loose screws on the front brake pad. It was an easy fix, all I needed was a specific Allen key, the exact kind of which I didn't have. I reflected that several people had said we had a few screws loose when we told them our honeymoon plans, and they appeared to have been proven right. I set about trying to tighten the screws with anything I could find. Scissors, a key, a matchstick. But nothing worked. Just when all hope seemed lost, Lady Luck decided that she had other plans for us.

Seemingly out of nowhere, a truck pulled up beside us. Two tanned and wrinkled farmers stepped out and gazed at us with amused smiles.

"*Vous avez un soucis*?" one of them asked, in a sentence that literally translates to "Do you have a worry?"

Boy, did we have a worry, we explained. We pointed to the wheel and tried to find the French words for "brake pad", "Allen key", and "screw" - none of which I knew at the time (and actually, none of which I know now).

"We saw you and your scooter as we drove past, and thought it seemed a bit bizarre, so we turned back to check up on you. That's our farm up the road," said one, introducing himself as Fabrice.

"Can you make it up there with the scooter? We can take a look, perhaps."

We wheeled the scooter along the road to their barn, and Farmer Fabrice was waiting for us with a perfectly fitting Allen key. He tightened the screws in mere seconds.

"You're the first Australian I've met," Farmer Patrick, his colleague, said to me. "And you're the first Swede," he told Lina.

As with all the other country folk we'd met, the farmers admitted that they had no time for Paris, and hadn't been there since they were children. Too many people, too fast, too much stress. Why would you live in Paris when you could live in the countryside, they wondered. Farmer Fabrice stood up, dusted off his hands, and said the job was done.

"And I have something for you, a little gift for the road," he said, jumping onto his pushbike and disappearing over the hill.

We were left with the other farmer, talking about our journey, Paris, and why my lips had peeled off. Farmer Fabrice returned with a glint in his eyes, concealing my apparent gift in his clenched fist.

Tenez, he said, take it.

I took the object, small, metallic, rigid, and I looked down to see the most valuable gift I've ever received - Farmer Fabrice's back-up Allen key.

"It may come in handy along the way," he said with a wink.

We thanked the farmers, noting how lucky we were that we had broken down so close to their farm.

"Lucky? Why, yes of course, you know where you are, *non?*" Patrick said. "You're in the village of Saint-Félix, he was the patron saint of good luck".

The sun was getting low in the sky and the farmers advised us to hit the road again if we were to make it to Verteuil before dark. We mounted the red beast, fastened our helmets, and prepared to take off. Farmer Fabrice had a parting message.

"I have one word for you: *merde,*" he said. (Which is French for *shit.*) "Don't ask me why, but in France, when we want to truly wish someone *good luck*, we just say *merde*. So, *merde,*" he concluded.

"Yes, *merde,*" echoed Farmer Patrick. "Now, get back on the road and don't lose that key."

With that, we pulled out of the farm and onto the road again, the scooter purring like a happy kitten. We had endless cornfields ahead of us and there wasn't a helicopter in sight.

8.6 The Brits

Did you know that a lot of Brits retire in the south of France? Many of them feel like they're maybe too old to get 100 percent into the "integrating" side of things and end up creating little English communities. As I understand it, a couple typically buys a place in a quaint little village, then lets their British friends use it as a holiday house when they're away. Those British friends become equally charmed by the lifestyle, then end up buying their own plot of land somewhere in the village too. Eventually, another Brit sees an opportunity and buys the local pub (or opens one) and sometimes even gives it an English name. Tourists from the U.K. will end up hearing talk of these little havens where the bartender speaks English and they pass through on a vacation and sometimes end up staying for life.

Now, I think it's wonderful what they're doing. Often they bring some much needed money, and I've read reports of some local communities crediting these Brits for the survival of their villages. But I'd never experienced this British phenomenon until we got to a place called Verteuil-sur-Charente, somewhere roughly east of La Rochelle. It was 150 kilometres inland and it put an unsightly dent in the side our lovely heart-shaped journey, but the village sounded just too enticing to miss. It was here that Jim, the Australian podcast listener, had his home and it was here we'd stay for a week. I'd always been curious about village life and had long wanted to experience it for more than just a day or two. This would be our chance.

Over the course of the week, we got to know everyone in the village. It turned out that Jim was something of a local celebrity, or at least that's how it seemed. Whenever we talked to a shopkeeper or cafe owner, they'd inevitably ask where we were staying and when we said "Jim's place" they'd beam and ask us how he was doing. We'd say that we'd never met him, and they were bamboozled by the story of his wedding gift. Then we'd get into talking about the podcast and the honeymoon and by the end of the conversation we'd feel like we'd made another friend in the village.

A British couple on the far side of town looked after Jim's home when he was away, and they'd greeted us with a bottle of wine. A few days later, they invited us to dinner at their house, where it felt like the whole Anglophone community had gathered. Over the coming days, we'd bump into them all at the local hangouts, and they'd introduce us to new people. The slower pace of life, the trust between the locals, it was all too good to be true - and such a far cry from the big city life we were used to in Paris. At one point, I got a haircut at the local barber and when it came time to pay I realized he didn't accept card payments. I had no cash, but said I could go and find an ATM.

"Ah, there's no cash machine in the village. Pay me when you can, no rush," he said.

By the end of the week, we had become locals. On our last night, one of the Brits in the village was having a blowout party for his 70th birthday and we'd been invited. It was surreal. We knew everyone, or at least that was how it seemed. There at the bar were Kev and his wife, our dinner hosts. Out in the beer garden was the Scottish couple. A British plumber we'd met at the local cafe offered us a glass of wine. And look, my hairdresser was talking to our favourite waitress at a table in the distance. It was all such fun, but it started to remind me of a movie ending where all the characters meet up in a dream after the main character dies. By the end of the night, just about all of the villagers had invited us back to Verteuil to stay with them at some point in the future. And we said we'd come.

As we packed up and hit the road again the next morning, I thought about how a week in a French village would suffice at this point in my life. Give me another thirty years, however, and I might just come back for good.

8.7 The accent

The first time I heard someone from southwestern France speak French, I got the giggles. I didn't mean to be rude, I really didn't, but it was just too funny. We were staying at a little bed and breakfast owned by a friendly lady with warm, kind eyes. She was so kind, in fact, that when she learned we hadn't eaten dinner, she brought us bread, eggs, and tomatoes from her garden. But what I'll remember most was her accent. She was pointing out a good path to wander along in her enormous garden. The word for path in French is *chemin*, which is pronounced in Paris like "sh-MAH". The sh should be short and the mah should be long and gentle. But that's not what the woman said. She said "sh-MENG". I'm not exaggerating, she literally said sh-MENG. But it wasn't just that. Her full sentence was that the path wasn't far (*loin*) away. The way I'd learned, the sentence should be "The sh-MAH isn't lwah". But she said "the sh-MENG wasn't LWENG". And when she said it, I'm ashamed to admit it I laughed. I thought she was joking.

"What did you say?" I asked.

And she repeated it. "The *sh-meng* isn't *lweng*". What the hell was going on?

"Why are you saying *lweng* and not *lwah*?" I asked, baffled at whatever game she was playing.

She took one look at me and laughed too.

"Ah, *jeune homme*, you've never met a Toulousain before?" she asked. "That's just how we speak down here."

And she was right. That's how they talked. Any of the words that have a gentle *ah* sound instead get a strange *eng* instead. And you hear it a lot. See you tomorrow, *à demain*, goes from *ah-de-mah* to *ah-de-meng*, bread (*pain*) goes from *puh* to *peng*, and the word for good, *bien*, goes from *bee-uh* to *bee-eng*. My favourite was when they put several together, like saying "tomorrow morning" (or "*de-MENG ma-TENG*"), which I thought had a fantastic ring to it. It doesn't even sound French; to me it sounded more Indonesian.

I later learned that this southern accent was often ranked as the most charming in France, even the sexiest. It's sometimes called *provençal*, or the language of Occitan, and is apparently a remnant from the old regional dialect. I found it fascinating and definitely charming, but I also found it very hard to see the sexiness in it, or to take it seriously.

I asked a policewoman in Carcassonne about it and she just raised an eyebrow. There's nothing strange about it, she said, which makes sense - no one finds their own accent unusual. I asked her if she would mind speaking into my microphone so I could give the podcast listeners a taste of this phenomenon. She agreed, and I scripted the following sentence: "*Demain matin, je vais acheter un pain au chocolat*" (Tomorrow morning, I'm going to buy a *pain au chocolat* pastry). My idea was with the *demain*, *matin*, and the *pain*, the accent would shine through. But she had the last laugh.

"*Ah mais non*, down here we don't call them *peng au chocolats*, we call them *chocolatines*," she said with a wink.

Ah, rumbled again. I noticed from that point on that no pâtisserie in the southwest made any mention of *pain au chocolat*. In fact, it's the only place in France where the famed chocolate-filled pastry is known by another name. But would a *pain au chocolat* by any other name taste as sweet? Yes, is the answer. The *chocolatines* were delicious.

By the time we left the southwest, I had fully embraced the *eng* and was using it with carefree abandon. If someone thanked me along the way, you could bet I didn't say *de rien* as I would in Paris. No way, I said *de rieng*, and I said it proudly. And nothing was going to stop me. *Rieng du tout.*

8.8 The Alps

We spent a few more breezy weeks driving through the south of France, which was every bit as wonderful as it probably sounds. We explored the small villages of Provence, the seaside towns of the Mediterranean, and the student cities like Bordeaux, Montpellier, and Toulouse. I learned that Carcassonne was the pearl of France for anyone with even a remote interest in history. All the while we were booking our accommodation one day ahead, sometimes even on the same day. It was a mix of AirBnB, hotel websites, and simply showing up at places and asking if there were any rooms available. And of course, we took up the occasional offers from lovely listeners who welcomed us into their homes. We even stayed in an old castle in Cognac and splashed out on my birthday at a fancy hotel with a Michelin-star restaurant downstairs. But for the most part, it was budget travelling. I was filming live videos along the way for the podcast members, and without them, we'd have had no income to continue the trip. I'd filmed live streams from the ramparts of Carcassonne and Saint Malo; while making galettes in Brittany; from a vintage car show in Angoulême; along the D-Day beaches of Normandy; and through the heart of Bordeaux. As we moved through the south we filmed from Montpellier, Roman arenas, and from the top of the famed Pont d'Avignon bridge. And we were blessed with good weather at every step of the journey. Lina and I were also doing weekly podcast episodes, discussing what we'd seen and giving recommendations along the way.

By the time we reached the northern part of Provence, we realized the warm weather wouldn't last. We only had one day of rain in two months - and we were well aware that if it got too cold or wet then it would be too dangerous to carry on. A farmer we stayed with in Normandy who collected motorbikes had taken one look at the tyres on our little scooter and had forbidden us to ever drive in the rain - or even when the roads were wet - and his warning had stuck with us. We set our sights on Annecy, a mythically idyllic Alpine town just beyond Grenoble, where we planned to have one last hurrah before tackling what would be the biggest challenge of the journey - crossing the mountains.

Annecy, for its part, lived up to the hype. It's the most beautiful town in France and I tell anyone who'll listen that you shouldn't leave France without visiting it. We were there in October, yet the skies were blue, the sun was out, and it was warm enough to take a dip in the transparent waters of Lake Annecy, which I did. It feels like you could point a camera at any angle and strike gold with that town. With its clear-watered canals, its Alpine backdrop, and the fairytale charm of its old town – it took us just five minutes to realize it was worth staying an extra night. But that may also have been because we knew the next day would be the hardest both physically and mentally. We were in the most mountainous part of France and couldn't get out without going up and over.

When it came time to leave Annecy, we filled the fuel tank for just five euros, as usual, but also filled up an empty plastic juice bottle with some extra gas, just in case we got stranded. We scrutinized the maps much more strategically than ever before, trying to find the roads with the least traffic, but crucially, the ones that had the gentlest inclines. The Red Beast had made it over 3,000 kilometres so far and we didn't want to push it any more. Worse, we didn't want it to die halfway up a mountain. The phone reception was terrible out there and we couldn't take too many chances.

It had also gotten cold. We'd been on the road for 55 days. The summer had ended, we were in October, and autumn had grabbed the countryside by both shoulders and given it a good shaking. The temperatures had dropped considerably, gone were the T-shirts and shorts, we rode with jackets, several layers of sweaters, and scarves.

And in tackling the mountains we had made up our minds up about one thing. If we didn't make it, we'd leave the scooter to rust on the side of the road as a warning to other scooterists foolish enough to take the same trip. Like Green Boots, the mountaineer who died on Mount Everest and whose body has marked the way for countless other climbers, Little Red could maybe be useful for years to come.

The journey was intense. The scooter struggled. When the mountains got to their steepest our top speed was around 10 km an hour (six miles). We sometimes drove in zigzags so the engine wouldn't stop. But while the ride was excruciatingly slow, it meant we could appreciate the stunning autumnal views. The wooded slopes blazed red and orange, the golden pastures stretched out below steep roadside cliffs. We stopped to drink from Alpine streams. But my favourite was the Peregrine Falcons that soared majestically above and kept us company through the deserted Jura Massif. Well, I like to think they were keeping us company. They were probably hoping for an engine failure and the rare chance to feast on Australian and Swedish meat.

In the afternoon we reached the summit right as the scooter sounded like it was about to breathe its last. We did it! We parked the bike on the side of the road, took off our helmets, and hugged one another. Even though we had been sitting all day, we were hit by such incredible fatigue - which had probably been accumulating over the past eight weeks. The downhill ride that followed was the sweetest of the entire trip.

We reached the town of Lons-le-Saunier on the other side of the mountains and the hotelier couldn't believe what we'd done. He kept repeating the details as we told him. You started in Paris!? Via Brittany?! You crossed the mountains?! For a honeymoon?! He upgraded our room to the biggest he had and sent up congratulatory drinks.

Lina and I, exhausted, unfolded our map of France on the bed and studied it once more. The plan had been to make a sweeping arc back towards Paris via the northeast of France, thereby exploring a new part of the country and tidily completing the other arc of the love heart shape. But as the sun set out the window and we sat on the edge of the bed, we decided that enough was enough and we instead planned a direct route back to Paris. The heart was a gimmick, and even though we'd based so many of our decisions on that silly heart-shaped route, completing it didn't seem important anymore.

In some ways, that day felt like the last of the journey, even though we'd continue for another week. We had driven 130 kilometres that day, which might not sound like much to you if you're used to travelling by car or motorbike, but for us it was a stupendous achievement. Tough driving conditions, perilous and unfenced ledges, and speeds as slow as 10 km, it was no wonder the hotelier was amazed. As for me, I was done. Absolutely wrecked. And so was Lina.

We plotted the route back to Paris with a rough idea of where we'd stay each night. While the carefree adventure was now (pretty much) over, we planned for a few memorable sights on the way home like some ancient caves and the pilgrim site of Vézelay. But make no mistake, we were done. We had conquered the mountains. The Red Beast was now The Alp Slayer.

And we slept very well.

8.9 The return

I knew we were officially back in Paris when I saw the other scooters. For two months, we were the only scooter on the road. Cars would beep their horns as they passed us, waving in delight to see us in the remote

French countryside. Other motorists would chat to us at gas stations. But the novelty was gone as we approached the capital from the south. It was strange to see how the city became so much denser from such a long way out. Cornfields turned into houses. Houses turned into buildings. Roads turned into highways. Traffic lights popped up more and more frequently. And there was traffic. Heavy traffic. And just like that, we no longer felt unique. We were back to being one of the pack. Two people in the glorious heap of a million. Sure, we had a story, but everyone did. This was Paris, after all.

We took a few victory laps around the Arc de Triomphe then headed to a friend's place to crash, and to crash hard. The friend was out of town for the week and we didn't have anywhere else to go, after all, since our apartment had been sold off while we were away. Meanwhile, the hotel prices in Paris were a rude awakening after two months in the countryside. That night we went to our local bar to meet our friends who we hadn't seen for months. And each of them, without fail, walked into the bar and said the same thing:

"I'll be honest. I was certain you wouldn't make it".

But we did make it. 4,000 kilometres, countless terrible hotel rooms, two months, one honeymoon. We'd scooted through the wild plains of the Camargues national park, where white horses and pink flamingos roam in green fields and on white beaches. We dined in Michelin starred restaurants and swam in the Mediterranean. We'd broken bread with village mayors, had numerous run-ins with local doctors, and three visits to the mechanic for repairs. I tasted cognac in Cognac, Bordeaux in Bordeaux, and Chantilly cream in Chantilly. We'd admired the ancient arenas of Provence, explored abandoned chateaux, and even stayed in one. I'd met fans, friends, and family along the way - and more kindly strangers than I could ever list. We'd scaled the ramparts in Carcassonne and Mont-Saint-Michel, dipped our toes in three different seas, and shared the view from the top of the Alps with soaring falcons.

In short, we'd seen France, the real France, the France that isn't Paris. And we could appreciate, well and truly, that it's a magnificent part of the world. The trip put the country into perspective, and as a result, it let me understand Paris and its people better too. Most French people in Paris aren't originally from the capital, and they often take great pride in talking about their hometowns and regions. Now that I was armed with the context from the trip, I felt I could understand the French a whole lot better. After all, as we had heard time and time again on our trip, we had probably seen more of France than many French people ever will. It wasn't an easy journey but we did it and it was wonderful. The scooter survived. And so did the relationship, thank God.

And for the umpteenth time in my Parisian life, I got ready for bed that night exhausted and I wondered what my next step would be. After all, we didn't have an apartment, our belongings were in storage, and we had no idea what the future held. As I got to bed, I saw Lina looking over the map from our trip and it turned out there was one last surprise.

She was drawing the last day of the journey onto the map, and she paused after adding the final stroke. She stepped back, turned her head to one side and furrowed her brow.

"You know," she said, "we may just have made the heart shape after all."

She took the map, which was almost as big as the bed, and turned it ninety degrees in a clockwise direction. Unbelievably, miraculously, we had indeed made a heart shape - and a rather impressive one at that. When we'd ducked inland from the west coast to visit the village of Verteuil, we'd fashioned a clear inward pinch or cusp at what was now the top of the heart. Annecy, to the east of France and on the opposite side of the country, was now the pointed outward pinch at the bottom. Paris and Marseille marked the outer edges, with the arcs now looping around Brittany and the southwest.

"It's a miracle, a romantic miracle," I said.

"It's a miracle that the scooter survived," she responded.

We'd been in Paris for almost four years now. The real miracle would be if we could find another apartment and make it to five.

CHAPTER NINE

Moving to Montmartre,
free drinks for life,
and one last party.

9.1 Montmartre

"You know," she said, lowering her voice and looking over her shoulder. "You could always bribe them. That's what we did."

My eyes widened. How exciting. How daring. How... infuriating.

I was sitting in a cafe on the Left Bank with a woman who'd finally found herself an apartment in Paris. She was an American, so was her husband, and they'd had enough.

"We'd been to 20 home viewings and no one ever called back. We got so sick of it that in the end we just offered the landlord an extra hundred euros a month. And it worked."

My mind raced. No wonder it's so hard to find a place, people are paying more than the asking price. How do the rest of us stand a chance? And we were already undesirables. If you lined me and Lina up against ten other people looking at an apartment, we may have just been the worst candidates. Two foreigners, neither with a full-time job contract from a French company, and lacking the infamous *dossier* - the series of papers proving that you earn the 'right amount' of money. Lina's shoe company was growing, but was still based in Sweden, meaning that I needed to prove that I earned over three times the rent per month... which I didn't. Not even close at that point. We already knew that we'd struggle to find a place after we'd been turned down for the drag queen's apartment two years earlier.

"You seem like such lovely people," the real estate agent said at the time. "But if you can't prove that you have a stable income from France then we just can't help you."

A British guy told me to forge a *dossier*. A Parisian said his accountant had 'modified' his payslips with a healthier salary. I knew it wasn't going to be easy, but this was ridiculous. It seemed the only real option was to buy a place, but unfortunately that was still a while away. So what are you supposed to do when you're competing with fraudsters, bribers, and the French?

One course is to play the same game, which I considered. The other is to rely on the network that I'd built over the past four years in France. It was the only way for us, really. I bombarded my social media platforms with posts about what I was looking for, sharing them in various housing groups and online pages. I explained that I was the kind of guy who loved paying rent on time and that Lina enjoyed nothing more than being tidy around the house.

And I got a lot of responses, which surprised us both. It felt like the tables had turned; we didn't have to prove ourselves like we would with a real estate agent. We were being invited to see apartments by people who wanted to have us there. Of course, there was an added danger to this approach: doing business without a professional middleman or woman can lead to all kinds of scams. But we were getting desperate. And to make matters worse, Lina, the standard by which I measure all things of good taste, was away in Sweden for work and I had to do it alone. Imagine the pressure! This wasn't just picking a restaurant, a movie, or a holiday destination. This was finding a home!

But hell, I live for challenges like this and I'd come a long way since I was too afraid to walk onto the basketball court. So I took to the apartment hunting with an appetite and criss-crossed the city looking for a home. And I suppose if it wasn't for the constant reminder that we were desperate, apartment hunting in Paris was rather good fun.

I got to meet new people who in some cases were being extremely kind because they were also desperate. One young couple, who contacted us because they thought the wording in our ad was so funny, poured me drinks and invited me to stay for dinner. They were heading to New Zealand for a year and couldn't find a reliable tenant. Their apartment was the best I saw, but it was *way* out in northwestern Paris, right on the edge of the city. I almost took it, but kept coming back to the thought: Why live in Paris if we're not going to be living *in Paris?* If we're going to be one hour outside of the action, would it really make any difference to live two hours out? Nantes and Bordeaux in western France were appealing to us after the honeymoon, and wildly cheaper than Paris. The thought crossed our minds to throw it all in and get a much bigger place out in the countryside.

Despite some very near hits, I still had no place and my time at an AirBnB in the north of the city was running out. As a last resort, I messaged a woman I vaguely knew who worked with holiday rentals - expensive ones though, the kind I couldn't afford. I told her my budget and she laughed. We were in different leagues, apparently. But a week later, she called to say a Frenchwoman had a place in Montmartre that matched my price. Montmartre, eh? Could we live in Montmartre? Despite four years in Paris at this point, I was no expert on what the locals call the village of Paris. I always considered it to be a little too far outside the city, a little too, well, touristy. But I could certainly take a look at the apartment.

This landlady, it turned out, hadn't yet advertised her property. She hadn't taken any photos of it either, which was no surprise. The Parisians are notoriously bad at photographing their own apartments. Sometimes you'll see rental photos with dirty dishes in the kitchen, untidy bathrooms, or people lazing on the lounge room sofa. I emailed the woman for more information and she told me that she needed a reliable tenant as she was moving to the suburbs. Apparently she was about to start a family and was in a hurry. She glossed over the practicalities of the apartment, a one-bedroom place on the fifth floor, and I said I'd come that afternoon.

So there I was, ready to visit yet another apartment, and once again flying blind with no idea what to expect. But this one felt different. Five floors up in Montmartre could mean anything. And Montmartre. The idea felt exotic to me. Romantic even. Montmartre, the *quartier* that had attracted young artists for decades. Perhaps the most charming part of Paris. But to live there? I looked up the address online, it was on a street right between the Moulin Rouge and Sacre-Coeur. The heart of Montmartre.

I headed over and found the building on an impossibly quiet cobbled road halfway up a hill (like most of Montmartre). I punched in the code, buzzed for the landlady, and she told me to head to the top floor via the stairs. There was no elevator (of course). I took the stairs two by two, marvelling at how five floors seemed so much more manageable than seven. But what, I wondered, would be behind door waiting for me on the fifth floor?

When I got to the top, the landlady was standing there ready. She was a young mousy woman, the kind who looked like she enjoyed getting lost in a good book. She dragged open the door and revealed a small and cluttered hallway. The bookish bit was right, books were planted like decorations on every surface. Folders and papers, everywhere. Stacks of them. I looked beyond the woman, who was beckoning me in, and the library theme continued throughout the apartment. And it wasn't just books. There were things, objects, everywhere. On closer inspection, the table in the hallway was actually a small piano. I glanced to the right, where a kitchenette was hidden by stacks of plates, pots, pans, and groceries. I tried to imagine where she chopped vegetables since there was no surface space. The bedroom over her shoulder looked like an overflowing vintage clothing shop. She didn't believe in storage, it seemed, or at least she preferred stackage.

"Excuse the mess, I'm right at the end of my final exams," she said, gesturing vaguely at the apartment. "But come in, come in."

I kicked off my shoes and followed her into the bird's nest of a lounge room. There were piles of books and CDs on the floor and two ankle-high tables in the centre that were cluttered with flowerpots, plants, mugs and more. Clothes were folded in piles on the sofa and the little desk in the corner looked like a stationery store that had been bombed. Even the walls were home to hanging clothes, hats, frames, masks, or rugs.

I was taking all this in while trying to keep up with the woman's rapid fire French. She asked where I was from and when I said

Australia she switched into perfect English. It turned out her mother was American. As we got to talking, I realized that she was a delightful person, perhaps just a bit stressed from her university exams. She was set to become a doctor and hadn't had time to think of anything but her books for months on end.

The shock of the clutter and the foreign language had thrown me, but I was soon back to my senses and wondering if the apartment could really work for two people. It certainly seemed too small, but was that just all the books? I tried to reimagine the rooms as if they were empty. I mentally added a cupboard or two, removed 500 books from the floors, got rid of the piano, and stripped the walls of everything. This could work...

One thing I really did like was the light. Even on a winter's afternoon, the place was bright thanks to the two ceiling-high French windows facing west. They looked directly into the building across the road, but there was a huge emptiness beside it, meaning a heck of a lot of light shone through. The landlady said that the windows in the kitchen and bedroom were facing east and gave plenty of morning light.

"And oh, you've not seen the view yet! I've forgotten the best bit," she said.

She opened one of the large windows, stepped through, and stood on a little balcony.

"Come, you can open the other window and have a balcony for yourself."

I hadn't even noticed the balconies, tiny little things, covered in plant pots. But I followed her lead and launched open my own French window and my jaw dropped.

With only a slight glance to my left, what seemed like the entirety of Paris was spread out before me. Thousands, tens of thousands of silver rooftops and red chimney pots stretched towards an uninterrupted view of the Eiffel Tower. Because we were halfway up a hill, the whole city was a good deal lower than where we were standing. It was as if we were in a hot-air balloon flying low over Paris. And this view could be mine?

My entire mindset changed from that moment. As we stepped inside again and took the full tour, I couldn't fault the place. Look at this, a bathroom with a full-sized shower! And fancy that, views from the kitchen and the bedroom too! And sure, at 35m2 it was a small place (375 square feet), but it was nearly twice the size of our old home in the 2nd arrondissement. I didn't need much more convincing; I told the woman we'd take it.

When she met Lina several days later to sign the documents, she said she hoped we would stay for a very long time. Yes, we were to live in Montmartre, the village of Paris. The setting for the Belle Epoque, where artists in the late 19th century gathered for low rent and cheap drinks. Where cabarets took the world by storm, where painters like Picasso and Renoir worked on their masterpieces, and where the legendary French singer Charles Aznavour based his most famous song, "La Bohème."

Two weeks after we signed the contract - and decades after all those famous faces had gone - we came screeching into Montmartre in a rented van with all our belongings in the back. We'd chosen to move mid-week to avoid the weekend traffic, but it meant none of our friends were free to help us. And because the deposit on the new place had cleared our bank accounts again, there was no budget for hired help. This was a shame, because I've always wanted to rent one of those crane hoists I'd marvelled at so many times in Paris. The ones that lift the furniture from the street right to the top window. If only! No, we did the bulk of the move alone. Lina took the wheel of the rental van for the white-knuckle drive through the narrow one-way streets, stopped at our new address, and I unloaded as much as I could before the traffic started to pile up. Then, with no space to park a car let alone a moving van, she took off and drove in a loop of our new neighbourhood as I bounded up five flights of stairs with four years' worth of belongings. It was insane and we were exhausted, but we did it with glee, knowing that our own little chapter was at the top of those stairs and ready to begin. Montmartre was to be on our doorstep. What a time to be alive.

9.2 The deal

One of the best parts of our new apartment was that it came with free drinks at the bar downstairs. Our landlady had made a deal with the bar owner so that he could store his beer in her basement, and in return, the apartment tenant would never pay for a drink. She told us that we had the choice: an empty basement or free booze. And we decided quickly. Realizing the lack of basement space probably explained her cluttered home, we decided to live as minimalists to avoid the same fate. And free drinks would come in handy after the wedding, honeymoon, and gargantuan deposit on the apartment had left us broke once again.

So, one winter evening after the final box was unpacked, we headed downstairs to introduce ourselves at the bar. And, as promised, the bartender said we didn't need to pay. For anything. Ever. He introduced us to all the regulars, topped up our drinks on repeat, and slid us bar snacks. We felt like celebrities that night and traded stories with our new neighbours. When eventually it was time for something more substantial to eat, we asked the bartender if he could recommend a restaurant in the area.

"Sure, there's a great one nearby. Do you want to eat now? OK, leave it with me," he said.

He promptly left the bar and walked out onto the street, leaving customers with change in their hands and wondering what was happening. When he returned, he said there was a table waiting for us just up the road. Slightly puzzled, we thanked him and headed for a meal, discussing on the way what was possibly in store. What could the bartender have said?

As we walked into the restaurant, a charming and authentic French spot, the waitress took us to the best table in the house. Two glasses of champagne appeared and the head chef came to introduce himself.

"I understand you're new to the neighbourhood, welcome," he said with a smile. "Allow me to recommend the *magret de canard* and the Pinot Noir."

We accepted the recommendation, but the chef had put us in a tight spot. The meal was among the most expensive on the menu and so was the wine, and our bank accounts were flatlining.

The good wine eased the pain. And so did the duck, which was succulent and served with a sweet potato purée. The chef, taking great pleasure in our visit, insisted on a dessert and produced a *crème brûlée* for two. I'm not ashamed to admit I was feeling more than a little tipsy. That first bartender had been refilling our glasses, there was the champagne... and what's this? The waitress had left the full bottle of Pinot Noir on the table. A full bottle? Good lord. I thought it was expensive just for a glass. Lina politely told the waitress that we'd only ordered two glasses, but the waitress just smiled, left the bottle, and moved on. I started to have flashbacks to Le Meurice hotel where the gin and tonics had left a hole in my pocket for weeks.

When the dessert was done, the waitress passed our table again. I decided enough was enough and nervously asked for *l'addition, s'il vous plaît?*

And she just smiled.

"*Ah, mais non, monsieur,*" she said. "Welcome to the neighbourhood. This one is on the house."

Over the counter in the kitchen, the head chef gave us a wink and a wave before returning to his work. We couldn't believe our luck.

As we headed home we popped back into the bar to thank the bartender for setting us up for such a marvellous experience.

"*Ah oui, mais c'est normale,*" he said with a smile. "That's what neighbours are for. Welcome to Montmartre."

9.3 Life in Montmartre

I love Montmartre. I never really had much time for it before, it always seemed too touristy, too far from all the action. And it was certainly too far to get to on foot because once you arrived, you were at the bottom of the hill and probably done with walking for the day. And it was even worse on a bicycle. But on the days we *did* make it there in the past, we were lost on arrival. We didn't know how to avoid the tourists, where to find the best bars and the quiet spots. It was only the locals and the tour guides who knew those secrets.

Despite the cold of our first winter in Montmartre, I was determined to learn the neighbourhood for myself. I walked endlessly. Even in the snow. Especially in the snow, actually. Snow in Paris is rare and made Montmartre look magical. I was there, filming live as dare devils took their snowboards down the hill of Sacre-Coeur. Gradually, I came to know every cobblestone in those empty streets near our apartment and beyond. In fact, Lina and I couldn't believe how deserted Montmartre was that winter. The tourists, of course, would return as the weather improved, but we felt like we'd discovered a secret part of Paris and we loved it.

By the time spring came around, I was an expert.

I had re-embraced my inner *flâneur* - heading deeper into Montmartre, over the hill and in every direction. Just like in my first days in Paris, back in the 2nd arrondissement, I couldn't walk enough. I had devoured the fascinating Montmartre cemetery, with its 70 stray cats and its unusual road-bridge ceiling. I found Picasso's studio, and knew which street to follow to find his old apartment. I stumbled upon hidden gardens and parks, a seemingly abandoned arena, and a fantastically empty cafe garden in the Montmartre Museum. And I found residential streets, like rue Félix-Ziem, with such breathtaking architecture that I'd wonder why anyone would want to be anywhere else. I raved about the neighbourhood on the podcast and developed a little tour route if listeners wanted to join me for a walk.

But it wasn't just the history, the tourist hotspots, and the hidden secrets that I liked. I made a special effort to introduce myself as a neighbour in all the nearby restaurants, bars, and cafes, and it had a wonderful effect. There are so many tourists in Montmartre that the locals often don't care much for first-time customers. But a neighbour? Why, a neighbour is a friend and should be treated as such. As the months passed, we found our favourite bakery, cheese shop, deli, cafe, and bar. And if the staff at a new place had no time for my neighbourly conversation, then *au revoir* to them. There were simply too many other places to try.

And I found my favourite street. Author Elaine Sciolino says that the only street in Paris is rue des Martyrs, but she's wrong. In fact, she went so far as to capitalize the words and make a book out of it, *The Only Street in Paris,* but it doesn't matter, she's still wrong. The only street in Paris is rue des Abbesses, which is around the corner from Elaine and by my doorstep. But why is it the best? Well, let me paint a picture.

The perfect Paris street must have all of the following things. At least one fantastic bakery. At least one good outdoor terrace for coffee or an evening drink. At least one decent restaurant. Plus, it must be gobsmackingly beautiful, with a sprinkling of interesting visual trinkets to keep your wandering eyes satisfied.

Rue des Abbesses had all of these things, often fivefold.

The street runs right through the heart of Montmartre, with one-way traffic heading from west to east. This means the street is fairly flat, as opposed to the north-south streets, which are mostly hilly. There are seemingly endless bars, restaurants, and shops at ground level, with a hodgepodge of vaguely Haussmannian apartment blocks above. Haussmann, who is responsible for the uniform beauty of Parisian buildings, never really got his teeth into Montmartre because the hill made it too tricky to raze and develop. Nowadays, the street is a goldmine for people-watching as it attracts all the locals for their daily fruits, vegetables, fish, cheese, and shoe repairs. Halfway along the street, there is a bakery that's famed for making the city's best baguettes, meaning they had the honour of providing the president with his daily bread.

And sure, there are scores of tourists keeping everyone on their toes, buying the overpriced ice cream, standing in the middle of the street and taking photos, and clogging up the sidewalks. But it's not like some of the other streets in Montmartre, where the shops sell tacky Eiffel Tower T-shirts and keyrings. There's an undeniable charm to Abbesses; it's like a classy village street and everyone knows it.

There is a definite community feel to the surrounding area too, the kind I'd heard about in Paris but hadn't experienced over my early years in the city. One day I popped into the local bakery for my daily delights and the baker trumpeted "And he's back from *les vacances!*" I hadn't even told her I was going away. The Moroccan guy at our local corner shop greets me by saying "*Salut l'australien*" as I walk past, which always makes me smile. "*Salut le marocain,*" I respond. I still don't know his name. When my local cafe closed for the summer, the staff members took a photo with me for their social media accounts. "We're doing it with all our regular customers, our true customers," one of them said. And sometimes, when we pass our local restaurants in the late evening, the waiters invite us in for a nightcap at the bar.

Yes, there is a real community vibe, and it thrives because of the flood of tourists. The changing faces visiting all these cafes, bars, and restaurants has made it all-the-more important to value the friendship of the locals. Surely helped by my incessant nattering away about being new to the neighbourhood, mixed with the locals' interest in an Australian-Swedish duo, Montmartre welcomed us and tucked us away in the fold. While elsewhere in Paris, I sometimes felt like I'd been chewed up and spat out, now it felt like I'd found my place.

And to be honest, it wasn't just Montmartre. Living halfway up the hill meant we were faced with a delightful daily choice. We could walk out the front door and turn right, up into the heart of Montmartre with all its cobblestone charm, or turn left and head down into Pigalle with its neon sins. I always thought it was funny to see how, at the top of our street, young women would parade along the charming rue des Abbesses, posing in front of the flower-laden restaurants. Meanwhile at the bottom of the hill young men with smirks on their faces would snap photos of the sex shops.

I preferred Pigalle for an evening stroll, among the young Parisians gathered on the bar terraces. The grittier streets, the raw personality, the vibrant nightlife. Montmartre was much better in the morning, with the bustle of the butchers and bakers, the cafe owners jostling between tables, and tourists walking around with mouths agape, experiencing the Paris of their dreams. It might sound strange, but I even liked seeing those tourists, especially when you could see how happy they were to be walking through the streets from their dreams.

But it wasn't all fun and games in our new lives. As our friends had predicted, Montmartre changed our habits. It truly was like a village and we didn't feel the need to venture into the rest of the city as much. Gone were the days of playing basketball in that wonderful covered market in the Marais. And the Canal Saint-Martin, which had hosted countless soirées over those early years, took a back seat as we preferred exploring new corners of Montmartre. I was no longer a regular at Le Peloton cafe, which was now on the far side of town as far as I was concerned. And, to my great chagrin, gone were the days of Lina's banana bread as our new kitchen wasn't equipped with an oven. Even our scooter, our beloved red scooter, retired from daily driving and only came out to cross town. We'd gone full *Montmartrois;* and we didn't mind at all.

9.4 The podcaster

Summer hit Paris hard that year. We suffered as the temperature reached 42.6 C (or 108.7 F), the hottest day in almost 70 years. And I can tell you, we were glad to see the end of the heatwave, not least after learning that zinc rooftops are apparently excellent at storing heat in top-floor apartments. But who was I to complain? It was some time during that summer that I had an important turning point.

Someone asked me what I did for a living and I answered, without hesitation, that I was a podcaster. Now that might seem quite a natural thing for me to answer, seeming it's true. But it was the first time I'd said it with absolute confidence. The first time I'd said it and meant it.

It was incredibly humbling that over 300 people were Earful Tower members. It was because of them that I kept doing it, and they gave me the faith to keep pushing forward. And they allowed me to have a salary. A job. My own job. Living my dream.

Besides the luxury of being able to pay for a lunch without searching my pockets for extra coins, having my own job changed me as a person. I wasn't chained to the rhythm of the news. I didn't have to work Monday to Friday, 9-6. And I could finally appreciate Paris for what it really was. I knew which cafes were empty during the week and perfect for holing up in a corner to write. I knew when the baguettes at the local bakery were still warm. And if there was a new exhibition in town, I didn't have to compete with all the Parisians to see it. I could stroll in on a Tuesday morning before even the tourists had arrived.

And all the while, the podcast was improving. As it grew ever closer to a million downloads, it became easier to attract guests. I didn't have to beg them for their time because they knew their message would be heard. The mayor of the fourth arrondissement in the Marais shared the chilling story of watching Notre Dame burn from up close. The mayor of Montmartre revealed for the listeners the hidden bar in the basement of his Town Hall. Supermodel and ultimate Parisienne

Caroline de Maigret took us all for a whirlwind walk around Pigalle. Author Cara Black jumped on the back of the scooter for a video, and the lead dancer of the Moulin Rouge invited us backstage. I was lucky enough to eat fresh biscuits in the kitchen of chef David Lebovitz and I almost fell off my chair to learn that John Baxter wrote the crocodile story into one of his own books.

And the real highlight was still on the horizon. Imagine my surprise when the Australian embassy agreed to let me host a live talk show at the ambassador's residence. I could bring 100 guests into his living room, in the most luxurious penthouse I'd ever seen, a stone's throw from the Eiffel Tower. The very thought made me tingle with fear and excitement.

But more on that later.

It seemed like I had come so far from when I arrived in Paris almost five years earlier, clueless and sorely lacking context. Now, radio stations and newspapers from around the world would ring *me* for the inside word on Paris. A radio host at the ABC in Australia became convinced that our honeymoon trip should be a movie and would call regularly. And somewhere along the way I even got my first sponsor for the podcast.

All this was a wild ride, but my favourite interactions have always been with the listeners. The lovely listeners. I heard that a table full of strangers met in Melbourne for an Earful Tower dinner at a French restaurant. Others have said they've listened to every show, which believe it or not would take longer than watching all the episodes of Seinfeld.

I hardly recognized myself compared to the man I was when I arrived. Then, I was too timid to speak French, to meet new people, to walk into restaurants. I didn't feel like I belonged and resigned myself to life as a curious observer on the sidelines. I knew no one, had no regular haunts in the city, and couldn't have pointed you in the right direction if I tried. Where once I was nervous to walk onto the basketball court, I now counted some of those *mecs* among my closest friends. I'd made Paris my home. I'd explored it so thoroughly that French friends asked me to take them on walking tours. I knew the history of the city but delighted in finding great new cafes. I'd seen Paris change a lot over those years too. I'd witnessed a coffee revolution, I'd seen the gentrification before my very eyes. And on a recent flight into Paris I'd noticed that they'd finally got rid of the telephone booths at Charles de Gaulle airport, which had stuck out so prominently on my arrival. Yes, I'd come to Paris on a one-way ticket and I managed, against the odds, to stay.

Long after we had settled in to our home in Montmartre, we decided to host a little soirée. A few hours before the guests arrived, Lina and I went to get some supplies from rue des Abbesses. We started with the champagne, ducking into our local wine store and asking for the shopkeeper's recommendation. We got chatting with him, in French of course, and said we were looking for two bottles of champagne. We traded stories about where we were from in the world and he said he was from Brittany. We surprised him when we said we'd scooted through his hometown. Our honeymoon story, now so well-practiced, left him shaking his head in disbelief. He had a scooter too.

When we got to the cheese shop, the *fromageur* was equally friendly. He shared his own stories about Sweden and Australia. He gave us a few samples, and laughed when I told him about my fear of cheese shops from years before. When we explained that we lived around the corner, he pulled out a loyalty card, stamped a few boxes, and said he hoped to see us again. We walked back home laden with the champagne and a haul of new cheeses to taste.

As we approached our little home on the hill, I had a major epiphany. I was reliving that night back in Montorgueil, when I'd invited my neighbour, Stephane, for cheese and wine. That first night, I'd been brushed off by the local merchants, had taken my cheese and wine back to an unimpressed neighbour, and we had eaten off a table made from a vintage suitcase. Now, I'd joined forces with the love of my life (Lina, not Stephane); we had picked good drinks and cheeses thanks to the lessons from the basketball *mecs*, and we lived in an apartment big enough to actually accommodate guests. And believe it or not, we had a proper table too. Yes, after years of being a struggling Australian in Paris, I finally felt like I was in sync with the rhythm of the city.

Later that evening, our friends arrived from their respective Paris neighbourhoods. Many of them hadn't been to our place yet, so we gave them the grand tour, which took all of 45 seconds. But still, we were proud that we had enough space and enough chairs for everyone. We popped the corks of the champagne and treated it like a housewarming party.

The highlight of the evening for our friends was the view of the Eiffel Tower. There's no denying it, the Iron Lady - especially at night - is a show stealer. At one point I was telling them all what I thought was a particularly funny story when the clock struck 10 pm and the tower lit up behind me with its twinkling light show, as it does every hour. The group ignored my punchline and pressed their faces to the window to watch. These were Parisians, mind you. They'd seen the lights. Probably many times. But they were drawn in like moths to this dizzying flame. Yes, the Eiffel Tower and its lights stole my thunder that night; but it gave me a cunning plan. A plan for how maybe, just maybe, I could use that tower to my advantage when the big event at the Australian embassy rolled around...

9.5 The embassy party

I still don't know why the Australian ambassador to France let me bring 100 people into his penthouse apartment. I also don't know why Australia, of all countries, has such a grand ambassadorial residence. And I had no idea, at the time, that the story behind my event there would be the last chapter of this book.

But now wasn't the time to be thinking about these things. It was late October, a crowd was arriving downstairs, and I was standing alone by the grand piano trying to figure it all out. I'd been in France almost five years and it seemed unbelievable to me what I was about to do. 100 people. In the flesh. For a talk show. That I was hosting. I'd never hosted a talk show before. Surely it was just like a podcast, right?

Now, the first thing you notice about the Australian ambassador's residence is that it's enormous. I mean truly gigantic. It's big enough to have at least one elephant wandering about without being a nuisance. Maybe even two. The second thing you notice is the view of the Eiffel Tower through the ceiling-high panoramic windows, looming so large that it feels like a fake Hollywood backdrop. The embassy is just 400 metres from that magnificent tower, and I was counting on the Iron Lady to provide a surprise grand finale for the evening... if only I could play my cards right. Yes, I had one last trick up my sleeve that would rely on impeccable timing, blind faith, and the courage to face certain embarrassment if things went wrong.

But for the moment, I was focused on the logistics of the night. The embassy team had set up rows of chairs on the ambassador's plush, thick carpet. The kind of carpet I imagine you could sleep on, if it really came to it. Carpet that felt comfortable on my feet even though I was wearing shoes. By the massive windows were two more chairs, a small table and two microphones. These were for me and my special guests; and this would be the stage for my first-ever talk show. With the wondrous Eiffel Tower right over my shoulder, I was calmed by the knowledge that if the talk show lagged, at least the crowd would have something worthwhile to look at.

The embassy had allowed me to host the talk show on the condition that it had an Australian theme. We decided on "Australians making their mark in France" and I invited guests including the lead dancer from the Moulin Rouge, author John Baxter, and Ambassador Brendan Berne (of course). We agreed to stream the show live for home viewers on YouTube and the embassy said all I was expected to do was put on a good show, fill the room, and provide the catering. The logistics and security meant it was like organizing a wedding in an airport, but a chance like this didn't come around too often and I was running with it. This would be Paris On Air, as no one had seen it before.

But back to the ambassador's living room. The evening was setting in, and the special guests were arriving. John Baxter channelled Al Capone, with a black overcoat and wide brimmed fedora. Amanda Chapman from the Moulin Rouge wore a short sequin dress and looked like she had stepped right off the stage. The ambassador himself oozed charm with an open jacket and a diplomatic smile.

Right before the audience arrived, we went over the plan. No more than five minutes per guest, short stories, on topic. A steady camera and a hidden timer in the front row. The ticking clock was the most important thing. We had to finish at 9 pm on the dot, not a millisecond later. I looked at the Eiffel Tower, blinking to life as the evening set in.

It was time.

The one hundred guests, no doubt eager to see the residence for themselves, flooded into the penthouse and the soirée began. And I wasn't ready for it. I was hit by an almighty sense of humbleness and nostalgia. About half of the crowd were my podcast supporters, the people who had truly believed in it and had joined forces to turn it from my hobby to my job. I recognized some of them from past events. Some had been listening for years. Some said they'd planned holidays from abroad to coincide with this very event.

In the crowd I also saw the faces from the past five years of my life in Paris. They streamed into the room in their best clothes as if it was a wedding. (Or a funeral - yet to be determined.) It was kind of like that final scene in *Titanic,* where all the characters are together one last time. My basketball buddies lumbered in, towering over the others. Friends, family, and even the guys from Le Peloton showed up too. Past podcast guests like Michael Kennedy from Paname Brewing Company and Nico Piégay from KB cafe were the catering heroes of the evening. And the local band Slim and the Beast, the guests from my very first podcast episode, brought their guitars and handled the entertainment. I spied other past podcast guests in the crowd too, like the Mayor of Montmartre and author Cara Black. But this was no time for mingling or thinking about *Titanic.* It was time for the show. I had it scripted to the second, we couldn't miss a beat.

As 8.30 approached, we gathered the guests into their seats and explained what was about to happen. Talk Show. Live Stream. Australian Theme. I started to sweat.

Gotta remember the clock. Can't waste a second. God damn that's a fine carpet.

I asked the crowd, if they wouldn't terribly mind, to cheer and applaud louder than ever before at the start of the show to spruce up the live stream. Then, I excused myself and headed onto the sweeping balcony with the ambassador for an opening monologue.

It was showtime.

The ambassador and I got the ball rolling, welcoming the home viewers on camera, then we headed through the balcony door into the living room. The roar of the crowd, playing along for full effect, was outstanding. It gave me the confidence I needed to fly through the show. And it all seemed to work. Each of the guests played their part: we talked about Australia, Paris, books, and cabaret. The clock ticked on. And with one minute until 9 pm, I got a signal from a helper in the crowd, who surreptitiously held up her phone with a timer ticking towards zero.

This is it. Here we go. One last surprise.

I started to give my thanks, in a speech I'd rehearsed so many times that I knew I could do it in exactly 60 seconds. I began by thanking the crowd and the sponsors. And everyone unexpectedly applauded.

What's going on? There's no time for clapping.

"Uh, please hold the applause," I urged in a panic.

60, 50, 40 seconds left.

My God, I'm running out of time.

I thanked the listeners, the viewers at home, my special guests. 30, 20 seconds. Out of the corner of my eye, I saw the head of the embassy team looking at his watch with wide eyes. He shook his head. He knew what I was about to do and had advised me against it.

Then... then... I looked at the crowd and I told them lie.

"I've organized a special thank you to the embassy, the ambassador, and the guests this evening," I said, focusing on the timer.

"I've spoken to the guys over at the Eiffel Tower and I said: Can you keep an eye on us tonight, and when I start clicking my fingers, maybe you could..."

As I spoke I raised my hand and clicked my fingers. And I didn't need to finish the sentence. Right on cue, the Eiffel Tower lit up with its mesmerizing show of brilliant, twinkling lights. 20,000 light bulbs flashing at once. From the penthouse view, from this close, it was almost as if we could feel the heat from them. It was pure magic. The crowd went wild.

Now of course, it wasn't *actually* me who made the lights sparkle. It happens every hour, on the hour, for a good five minutes, as you well know. It's one of the most regular wonders of the City of Light that everyone should see before they die. But to this day I still get the occasional email asking if I *really* was in cahoots with the Eiffel Tower staff.

No, it was just perfect timing, and the guests at the soirée knew it too. But it had the right effect: they oohed, aahed, they took pictures, and applauded - and it was the ultimate end to the talk show.

As the applause faded, my nostalgia set in again. I stood back and took it all in, reflecting on the whole crazy ride of my time in Paris. My mind flashed back to when I had seen the same Eiffel Tower light show five years earlier, alone in my communal seventh-floor toilet. I thought of my Valentine's Day with Lina under that same tower; a delightful date that had paved the way for a marvellous marriage. And I thought of our home in Montmartre, on the horizon, where we so often watched the same light show as if for the first time.

At the back of the penthouse living room, I spied Lina, the love of my life. I smiled. And she smiled back. We were five years into our story but it felt like it was just beginning. Over my shoulder, countless grey rooftops and terracotta chimney pots stretched off into the distance. And the Eiffel Tower continued to sparkle.

ACKNOWLEDGEMENTS

Writing a book like this isn't possible without help. Quite a lot of help, it turns out. Thanks to my wife, Lina, for being my sidekick, and often the instigator, in most of the stories you've just read. Thanks to John Baxter for reading the first draft, Paul O'Mahony for editing the second, and Janet Hulstrand for adding a magical grammatical polish that I didn't even know existed. And thanks to photographers Danielle Nicole, Anna Mardo, Amber St. Lucia & Janelle Sweeney.

Thanks to the guests who've been on my podcast, the people who've listened to it, and especially all the kindly folks who've become Patreon members and allowed my hobby to become my career.

But most importantly, this first edition was made possible largely thanks to the following people. Their generosity during the Kickstarter crowdfunding campaign made all the difference. And without them, no one would be holding this book. *Alors, un grand merci.*

Ruth & Peter, Tom & James, Eddie & Elizabeth, Mary Barone, Joan Burns, Lida & Reed Randolph, Kim Loftus, Sandy Esteve-Ziegler, the Moores & the Pearsons, Maria Trenzado, Blythe & Marc Musteric, Deborah & Ron Ball, Nan & John Moss, Judith Solanki, Meredith Mullins, Lu Brigham, Terry Cardwell, Shelah Miner, Lachlan Cooke, Steve Oswald, John Clarke, Lynnelle, Cindy Owens, Jodee & Carl Boehm, Juan Ulloa, Jim Carmichael, Katherine V. Miller, M.D., Camille & Olivier from FrenchToday.com, Philippe Hertzberg from SecretJourneys.Travel, Erin & Michael Bittler, Christine Gitomer, Margaret ("Maggie") Patterson, Cindy & Melanie Mollard, Dimetrios & Samantha Kantzios, Joshua Swanson, Human Nature, Cindi Witfoth, John & Ana Margolles, Heidi & Michael Boyd, James Arthur, Franc & Sandra.

ABOUT THE AUTHOR

Oliver Gee was born in Melbourne, Australia. At the tender age of 21 he left Australia seeking adventure in Africa and Europe. He tried and failed to settle in London, very nearly settled in Sweden, and seems to have settled in Paris.

He runs the award-winning travel podcast The Earful Tower, which you can find anywhere that plays podcasts. To learn more about Oliver, a good place to start is theearfultower.com.

Oliver finds it difficult to write in the third person, and wonders why anyone would read an "about the author" section of a book that has largely been about the very same author.

Paris On Air is his first book.